PRAISE FOR JO CAULFIELD

'There's so much I'd like to say about this book. It's a wildly satisfying and moving read. Big laughs combined with rare insight and heartbreak. The writing is so readable and unfussy and the humour is done so well, never forced or shoehorned. I loved this special book.'
GRAHAM NORTON

'Where do you start with the death of a beloved sibling? I wish I'd started on page one of Jo's book. She navigates the treacherous waters of bereavement and its unpredictable behaviour and emotions in this open, funny and highly readable gem . . . A literary lifebelt for the bereaved'
JO BRAND

'I knew Jo Caulfield was funny, one of the funniest comics around, but her book is also moving and surprising. A brilliantly engaging read'
SUSAN CALMAN

'Laughter isn't just for the good times. Laughter is what gets us through the toughest times, and Jo Caulfield demonstrates that beautifully in this heartfelt and hilarious book'
JIMMY CARR

'Warm and tender, frequently very funny and, ultimately, incredibly moving tale of siblings and cancer. Without a shred of mawkishness, the book manages to move seamlessly from funny to tragic'
JENNY ECLAIR

'Sweet, brutal, funny, intimate and totally compelling, this is a brilliant meditation on grief and sisterhood – and a celebration of the seemingly inconsequential details and random moments that bind us to each other'
VIV GROSKOP

'I was blessed to sit in a room making up jokes with Annie Caulfield. Jo has captured her big sister's sense of humour and humanity beautifully'
LENNY HENRY

'If this book was just a eulogy, that would be more than enough reason to say that you must read this, but it offers readers so much more. It is an inspirational book about love, fragility, loss and the bond between two sisters. Captivatingly told and filled with enchantment, it made me glad I had known Annie and glad that I know Jo'
ROBIN INCE, *THE INFINITE MONKEY CAGE*

'I devoured it in one sitting. Loved it: funny, warm, engaging'
EMMA KENNEDY

'Jo's writing is a master-class in letting the catastrophe of loss speak for itself. Amidst heartache and grief shines the joy of the extraordinary sibling bond, so often taken for granted. A super read'
SHAPARAK KHORSANDI

'Excellent writing with heart, truth and comedy rolled into one important journey'
HELEN LEDERER

'Moving and wry'
IAN RANKIN

'A beautiful, bold portrait of a much-loved sister that will speak to everyone who has loved and lost and everyone who is yet to lose someone. Honest, raw, surprising, life-affirming, and because it's Jo Caulfield, of course, it's very, very funny. You'll laugh, cry, breathe and want to read it again'
DEBORAH FRANCES-WHITE, *THE GUILTY FEMINIST*

Annie Caulfield, a very grown-up eighteen,
and me, a very young thirteen.

The Funny Thing
About Death

Jo Caulfield

love & thanks

Jo Caulfield.

Polygon

First published in Great Britain in 2023 by Polygon,
an imprint of Birlinn Ltd

Birlinn Ltd
West Newington House
10 Newington Road
Edinburgh
EH9 1QS

www.polygonbooks.co.uk

1

Jo Caulfield will make a contribution of all profits she receives from the
sale of this book to Macmillan Cancer Support. This is estimated to be
at least £8,000. Registered charity in England & Wales (261017),
in Scotland (SC039907) and in the Isle of Man (604).
Also operating in Northern Ireland.

Excerpts from *Irish Blood, English Heart, Ulster Fry* and
The Winners' Enclosure are reproduced here with the kind permission
of Martin McNamara. 'Busy Doing Nothing', 'Rock 'N' Roll Suicide
and Ashes to Ashes', 'Unusual Places to Live', 'Annie Caulfield's Guilty
Pleasure', 'One Little Dot', 'Name Dropping for Charity', 'Atonement',
'Sports and Games – Just for Fun?' and 'When I Grow Up' were
originally published in *Standard Issue* magazine and are reproduced
here with kind permission.

ISBN 978 1 84697 635 3
eBook ISBN 978 1 78885 591 4

British Library Cataloguing-in-Publication Data
A catalogue record for this book is available on request
from the British Library.

Typeset by Initial Typesetting Services, Edinburgh

To my brother James Caulfield

Contents

Contents

1

David Cassidy and Other Stories

Three siblings on a plinth doing
God knows what, 1970.

She was four and a half years older than me so I've never known a world without Annie. She was already here, ahead of me, being exciting, inventing games and making up stories. One of my earliest memories is of lying in bed and Annie pointing into the sky on Christmas Eve. 'There's Santa and his reindeers,' she said. I jumped up to see them and there they were, Santa on a sleigh soaring through the starry night sky. Who needed hallucinogenic drugs when your older sister could make you see things?

The power of a big sister is mighty but it makes for an unreliable narrator. Purple Smarties were poisonous, the Virgin Mary appeared to her in the bathroom, if I cut my hair it would grow back blonde (I did, and it didn't) and David Cassidy was her brother – yes, seventies TV's David Cassidy. He was busy filming *The Partridge Family* but visited her whenever he could, she said. It seemed logical. Who wouldn't rather live in California than on an Air Force base in Norfolk?

I soon realised that I should believe much of what Annie said in the same way that I believed Shirley Jones was David Cassidy's mother. I knew it wasn't true but it didn't stop me enjoying the show.

Everett Collection/Alamy

★

Storytelling/lying is quite a skill; you can't just jump into it. I learned this lesson early in life – a very valuable one considering that years later I would become a comedian. Conditions need to be right: you need to know your audience.

When I was about six years old, Annie ten or eleven and our brother James eight, we were playing on a bit of wasteland on the RAF camp. The ground was muddy and had dried hard into a crazy-paving pattern. James and I were following Annie, putting our feet neatly onto each dry slab, trying not to touch the edges. That was the game. This was a familiar order in our childhood: Annie, James and then me. Annie said, 'Don't leave your foot on too long, or the cracked edge will separate and you'll fall all the way down to Africa. You'll land in the Sahara desert.' What an amazing thought. I could completely imagine this piece of dry mud whooshing down cartoon-style through the earth and then suddenly popping up, with me on it, in Africa. In fact, *Journey to the Centre of the Earth* was one of my favourite films at the time. I had loved the scenes of people walking through galleries of molten rock. We all hopped much more quickly from one slab to the next, now with the added danger of being whooshed to Africa. It was that non-threatening danger that made you slightly hysterical with laughter. Laughing would slow you down, which made you laugh even more as you knew you had to keep hopping, but you couldn't keep hopping because you were laughing so much.

A little while later I was playing in that same area without Annie. I was with Julie and Dawn Troughton, who lived across from us and were a bit younger than me. I told them about the cracked crazy-paving mud and how it would open up and we could end up in Africa. But it didn't work the same way as when Annie said it. They went crazy. Julie became hysterical, but not in the good, laughing way. Then, as she stared, terrified, at the screaming Julie, Dawn started frantically yelling, 'Get me off! Get me off!' The grassy area was only about twenty feet away, but Dawn just kept jumping up and down on the spot. Which, if the story had been true, was *exactly* the wrong thing to do. I told them it was made up, that it wasn't true, but they wouldn't believe me. They just kept bawling, so I had to physically pick up Dawn and half drag, half carry her to safety. I lay on the grass waiting for them both to calm down so we could play some more, but they wanted to go home.

Next thing I knew, their mother was glaring at me like I was some kind of maniac. 'Why would you say such a horrid thing, Jo?'

Julie was still crying, rocking back and forth – Jesus, it was just a story! I knew it was a story when Annie said it to me, so how did they not know it was a story? A scary, fun story. 'But that's not fun, Jo – that's very frightening. Do you think Julie is having fun?' said her mother. I thought Julie was a fucking idiot.

How had it all gone so wrong? Had these boneheads never been told a story by their older sister? One that you both absolutely believed and went along with, but which you also knew wasn't true. This storytelling malarkey was harder to pull off than I'd thought. Apparently you needed to choose your audience carefully; these pathetic weaklings were clearly not my audience.

2

Blam

Oswaldtwistle (pronounced Ozzel-twizzel): that's where I was when I found out that Annie was ill. I was in the middle of a stand-up comedy tour. I thought the name sounded like a character from Dickens – 'Mrs Ozzle Twizzle, always fussing and will never get her inheritance' – but it's actually an old mill town that had been the home of James Hargreaves, the inventor of the Spinning Jenny. This was a fact that had lain dormant in my brain since O-level history, and it made me strangely excited to be there, like meeting a celebrity. The Spinning Jenny man. My show at Oswaldtwistle hadn't sold well so I'd booked myself into the poshest hotel in the area – I like to double down on financial disaster if ticket sales are slow.

The hotel room was one of those ones that looks good but is actually completely impractical and badly designed. Design has nothing to do with price. Cheap chain hotels like Travelodge and Days Inn have very well designed rooms. (Ibis have those weird, moulded bathrooms that, although perfectly functional, always make me feel that I'm on a cruise ship – a cruise that is way off course going through Doncaster.)

I've come across these hotels before and they have a few tell-tale signs. They usually make them look ultra-modern with minimalist decor and an orange chair and something weird in the reception like a fluorescent owl. The room lighting is on a 'lighting pad' – some sort of stupid touch screen that is so much more complicated than a light switch – and the bathroom is described as a 'wet room'. This room had one of those wall-mounted hairdryers that looks more like a prototype of an early DustBuster and emits a thin, lukewarm breeze. After hitting my funny bone on the wall – which I couldn't quite see because of the dim lighting – I ricocheted from wall to sink to toilet and then fell back onto the bin with the hairdryer still in my hand but now unattached to the wall.

A lot of these rooms are designed by men who think you can wash your hair in the shower. Contrary to all those shampoo ads where women languidly lather their hair and have orgasms, it's actually quite difficult to wash long hair in a shower. What I want is a sink. A classic, old-fashioned sizeable sink. Not a thing that looks like a Japanese water fountain or a glass bowl. The number of times I've nearly broken my neck or inserted a tap in my ear because I'm trying to squash my head into what appears to be a Barbie Doll sink . . . Stop fucking with the design – the traditional sink is perfect.

But, in Oswaldtwistle, I was glad I'd splashed out on a nice hotel. It would have been so much more miserable and lonely to be staring at the pale blue walls of a Travelodge when I found out that my big sister had cancer.

I noticed an email from Annie and thought, I'll have to tell her about Mrs Ozzle Twizzle; she'll love it, and the death-trap bathroom . . .

From: Annie Caulfield
To: Jo Caulfield
Sent: 28 February 2015
Subject: Blam

Well all is well and funny and nice apart from this one arse of a thing. Don't know what's best but I thought an email would mean it wasn't all 'blam' and alarming. The back pain weirdness turns out to be a bit of cancer in my right lung, so it has been pressing against nerves. Treatment starts this week, v. optimistic as I'm so otherwise healthy. So I don't stay in hospital or anything, just trot down the road and come home again and not every day.

I am very settled into the idea now so do call when you're ready and tell me more about your friend's Guardian Dates!

Spoke to James; he agrees that telling the parents will just be a nightmare so am leaving that for another week or so. I think Mother has enough on her plate and he will just find some way to make something I'm fine with into something awful.

So it's just 'a health setback' as my gloriously camp chemo nurse says, but thought I'd better say . . .

Talk soon x

I sat on the hotel bed monitoring myself for a reaction. I honestly didn't have one; it was all too unknown to me. That's fine, I thought, no point manufacturing a reaction. Look it up online. That's the thing to do.

The websites I found said all sorts of things about 'stages' and that people died, and something in me realised that this wasn't a good idea. Also, what's the point of me looking it up? Am I going to think of something the oncologist hasn't? 'Excuse me, doctor of many years' experience and training, I've just skimmed through this NHS website and I may have come up with something . . . yeah, think I've got a few ideas.'

At almost exactly the same time, I got another email from Annie telling me not to look it up online. 'There are so many variables linked to age, health and lifestyle that you can't gauge how you will be affected.'

Those two emails say so much about Annie and how she was going to deal with having cancer. It made me think of the French and Saunders characters, the 'Country Ladies', who would chop off a finger by accident and go, 'Oh, stuff and nonsense, just a finger. Let's not make a fuss.'

This was 'a health setback'.

Not that Annie was a Country Lady. Definitely not. She thought the country was 'full of racists baking bread and writing their fucking blogs'. Annie and I enjoyed making sweeping judgements about people; well, everyone needs a hobby and I don't bake. Oh, and 'the *Guardian* Dates' are literally that; a friend had joined the *Guardian*'s dating site thinking it would be full of nice liberal leftie men, but it turns out they can be creepy arseholes, too.

The emails told me that she had already made herself okay with this news. And also that she would control the narrative. Facts would be altered to make a better story or fit how she wanted to present herself to the world, as she had since childhood.

About five minutes after reading the email I phoned her. I let her talk and tell me about the treatment plan. I didn't feel anything particular because I had no idea what I was dealing with. Cancer is not one thing, with one prognosis, one result, so to act like it's a huge tragedy is just being dramatic. You don't know yet.

She said she had known for over a week. What had that week been like? What had she thought? I didn't know, I didn't ask, but I was curious and perversely fascinated by what that felt like – completely inappropriate thoughts. I didn't know what I was supposed to do. Be supportive, obviously, but how? And . . . I had to go, I had a show to do. She laughed at that. 'How rude. I've got cancer and "sorry, got a show to do" – worst sister ever.'

When I arrived at the venue the staff told me that they'd invited family and friends to make up the numbers. My stand-up persona has been described as 'acerbic and high-status': that's difficult to pull off when everyone at the venue feels sorry for you because you haven't sold many tickets. They offered me cake, and then when I said, 'No, thanks,' they said, 'Oh, good, we don't have any.' That immediately made me laugh. This is going to be a good show, I thought, I'm going to be okay. Afterwards I was filled with a love of humanity – comics will say they loved an audience and we genuinely mean it, in our way – but my love of humanity quickly faded. Very soon after the gig I reverted to my usual prickly self. I went back to the hotel to re-read Annie's emails.

An email rather than a phone call is a good way to find out. It gives you time. The sender doesn't have to deal with your immediate outpourings of emotion. I see now that Annie was almost paralysed by the fear of how people she loved would be upset by her illness. She needed us all to keep our upsetness to ourselves.

She had chosen not to tell our parents yet. You might think that weird, but really, what would've been the point? My mum was busy up in Leicestershire looking after my dad, and she was eighty-five – what could she do but worry? She couldn't leave my dad on his own, and the logistics of getting her to London would have been too stressful for everyone.

Despite generally being a gossip, I learned that I am good at keeping a secret. I didn't tell anyone except my husband. I didn't even tell my best friend Adam. Adam knew Annie well, but our mothers play bridge together. I knew Adam would tell his mum, and it wouldn't be fair if Adam's mum knew but mine didn't.

I had Martin, my sister's partner, and my brother to talk to. Other than that I just locked the knowledge away. This was serious.

My brother James and I had the first of scores of discussions about the rights and wrongs of not telling our parents. In the end we decided it wasn't ours to tell, that we had to respect what Annie wanted. Didn't we?

James is a Catholic priest. Yes, quite different to Annie and me; he's a chaplain in the RAF, although he does 'perform'. He says he can tell if he's losing the crowd in a sermon and needs to throw in a joke or cut to the chase: 'And so Jesus was right again. Amen.'

He has always respected our right to not believe and we respected his right to believe. It's odd as fuck, but I also think it must be wonderful. To actually have faith, to believe in God and Heaven and all that comforting malarkey. Do people really believe in Heaven? A place full of all the dead people. David Bowie, Charlie Watts and Kirsty MacColl all hanging out together. And putting aside my horror of the institution of the Catholic Church, James is not the Catholic Church. He is my brother, a person with this magical, inexplicable thing – faith – who's trying to do the right thing.

A priest, a writer and a comedian walk into a bar . . . it's a family reunion.

11

3

So Much Love for John Lewis

A for Annie.

A couple of days after the phone call, I went down to London and met Annie at Peter Jones department store, one of our favourite places for tea and judging people. Peter Jones is owned by John Lewis, so if you're a John Lewis lover, that's all you need to know. I've often thought that John Lewis should run the world. They are good to their staff and were one of the first companies to give same-sex partners the family staff discount. Sort of socialists, but also they understand that we still want to have nice things and go for tea and cake. I live in Edinburgh now – we moved here from London on a whim about ten years ago – and it's an ideal size. You can walk everywhere. From the same spot I can walk to the sea, have a view of a mountain and be ten minutes on the bus from John Lewis. What more can you want from life?

Annie was shockingly thin. Bones sticking out, arms with barely any flesh on them. Oh God, how did she get so thin? How could we have let her get so thin? I thought about another day when I'd met her in Soho. I'd thought then that she was looking thin – when was that? It was warm and sunny, was it last spring? It could have been over a year ago. I hadn't said anything; I didn't know that weight loss is a huge sign that something is wrong, something like cancer. She had cut out carbs and sugar. I knew she liked being thin, but she was too thin. It had been disturbing at the time, and I think about that over and over again. What if I had said something way back then?

'You're too thin, Annie, you should go to the doctor.'

Why didn't I say something? If I had, could they have found the cancer earlier? Or was the thinness nothing to do with cancer?

She asked if I minded going to the counter, as she was too weak. She wanted a cream cake and a hot chocolate – she was under instructions to eat whatever she wanted and put on weight. She was still finding her feet in her new role as a person with cancer. That's how she seemed, like an actress. Yes, she had cancer, but *how* was she going to have cancer?

The worst thing in life to Annie was to be boring.

She wanted to do this well, to be a person with cancer in the best way she could; it was her own peculiar kind of bravery. She was always brave, all her life, because she would be scared and worried and usually unprepared but she'd just take a breath and charge ahead. They are the really brave ones, the scared people, not the sporty warriors who go bungee jumping and white-water rafting. I can see her small head, the short blonde hair, see her face thrust forward, grabbing life, worried but wanting to be one of the brave people.

★

There were many things I questioned, but I just pushed the questions away. They didn't help. Regression, that was my solution – I would go back to how I was as a kid, when Annie knew best. For years I trotted along behind her, just happy to be there. But over time I had realised that 'knowing' wasn't the most important thing to Annie; too much planning and research meant you probably wouldn't do something. The *doing* was what was important because that would make something happen, something you could learn from, something that would take you to a different world. Something you could write about.

When I was sixteen and she was twenty-one, we went hitchhiking around Europe. Not Inter-railing – hitchhiking. Getting in strangers' cars. Two young women alone, it did occur to me that maybe it wasn't a great idea, but Annie knew best. It was only when we were jumping out of a moving lorry as it slowed down on a hairpin bend in the Swiss Alps that I thought, 'Maybe Annie doesn't always know best.'

We were sexually harassed across five countries, but you don't get good stories by making sensible decisions. In France we got a lift from a handsome older man. Annie sat in the front and chatted away in French, some of which I understood. He then drove off the main road into a wood. Then he drove further into the wood. Driving young women into a wood is classic horror-movie stuff. It's Little Red Riding Hood, for fuck's sake. It's clearly a bad sign. Alarm bells were clanging in my head.

The road became a dirt track. I whispered to Annie that we should stop or ask him where we were going. I could tell Annie was worried, but she didn't want to let on, she didn't want our adventure to go wrong. He stopped the car, saying this was an excellent place to camp. We watched him drive away.

Maybe it *was* a good place to camp – alone, deep in the woods, about three miles from the nearest main road, just as it was getting dark . . . Annie seemed to think it was fine, so I acted like it was fine. We started to put up our tent and talked about how the man had looked like Clint Eastwood. Very handsome. I looked up and there he was, about a hundred yards away.

'Annie, he's back! He's coming towards us!'

Annie looked up at Clint Eastwood. She went forward to speak to him. They exchanged a few sentences, and then she swore at him. I stood behind her clutching a saucepan, ready to step in if the reasoning in French didn't work. '*Que a la main*' – I picked out that phrase – did it mean just a hand job? He was gesturing and shouting as though he was complaining about bad service in a restaurant. One last Gallic shrug and he turned round and went off down the track. Annie turned to ask if I was okay, laughing and hugging me when she saw the saucepan. How different our reactions were – maybe I have always been more of a saucepan-wielding realist. It makes my heart ache to think how young and inexperienced we were, but she looked out for me, always putting on a brave face.

The 'Bad Clint Eastwood', as he was then referred to, had put some money under a windscreen wiper when he picked us up. Apparently that was a sign, and we should have known that he was going to take us into the woods and get a blowjob, or some sort of job.

We discussed the likelihood of him coming back. Bad Clint Eastwood knew where we were. We packed up and made the long trek down to the road. I thought every approaching car was him coming back. I was helpless with fear and laughter as my sister whispered, 'It's Bad Clint Eastwood, it's Bad Clint Eastwood,' until the car disappeared from view. 'It's not Bad Clint Eastwood.'

It was night, and we didn't have anything sensible like a torch so we were stumbling around in the dark not quite sure where we were. I don't remember setting up the tents, but we thought it was sensible to move 'inland', away from the roadside. We woke to the sound of bulldozers. Looking out of the tent in daylight, it appeared that we had camped in some sort of quarry. It was very much a working quarry, and we were perched on the very edge of it, on a tiny square of unexcavated land. Men in hard hats were stomping about only twenty feet away, and Annie was casually doing her usual morning routine of cleaning her face with Anne French Deep Cleansing Milk. The smell of lemon and damp sleeping bags.

Later in the trip we somehow ended up back in the Alps, wearing shorts and hitching by the roadside in the snow. We had failed to collate the whole higher altitude/lower air temperature weather thing. We were freezing cold, and I'd missed breakfast, so I was sure I would be dead by lunchtime. Having adventures and stories to tell was losing its appeal. Salvation came in the form of two young Japanese men in a tiny Fiat. They showed no desire to do any raping and instead fed us biscuits and put jumpers on our legs. Annie did know best.

She approached cancer much as she had approached that trip. Too much research and knowledge might not be the way to go. I think she may have realised very early on that her chances were slim – I will never know. She didn't need to know the worst-case scenario. She certainly didn't need or want anyone talking about *her* cancer.

4

It Was *Her* Cancer

Cancer was suddenly everywhere. People couldn't shut up about cancer. There seemed to be endless celebrities talking about their 'battle with cancer'. I shouted at people on TV, 'You're not the only one with cancer! My sister has cancer.' I know, ridiculous.

There is no right or wrong way to deal with having cancer. A lot of people do it very publicly. They will make a diary of their treatment, do a blog or put everything on social media. They will be almost aggressively positive and open, sharing all the details. But that's not the only way, and I feel strangely defensive of my sister because she didn't deal with it in that way. I got irrationally annoyed with all the openness about cancer. Somehow, if you weren't being open and sharing, you weren't 'playing the game'.

It felt like a personal attack on Annie, this *One Show* approach to people with cancer. 'So, today we have a person with cancer on the show . . . Tell us how brave and positive you're being, and be funny about anything unpleasant, and crying would be good too – but not too much as that's not really the feel of the show and the next item's about Gino D'Acampo's new cookbook.'

Cancer was the least interesting thing about Annie. It wasn't her; it was something that happened to her. I resent giving it attention. Cancer doesn't care who you are. Even arseholes get cancer. Remember when Lance Armstrong got cancer and everyone loved him, but then we found out he was a bully and a cheat? Having cancer doesn't automatically make you a hero. It's patronising and belittling, this canonisation of people because they have cancer. Cancer doesn't reward you for researching it or investing your time and energy in trying to beat it. You are nothing to cancer, you're just a place to stay. It may leave you, never to return, or it may come back again and again, or it may ravage you quickly and thoroughly. Cancer doesn't care who you are: it is random and merciless. She was so much more interesting than cancer. But cancer ended up being the dominant storyline.

Annie separated herself from the cancer by putting complete faith in her oncologist Dr Tom. Not just to cure her, but to protect her. He would deal with it. She chatted about Dr Tom like he was her very clever friend, who just happened to be a genius about cancer. How handy was that?

Martin, her partner, said he realised why oncologists are so special. They really do treat the whole person. They have to judge how much truth people can take. I think Annie could take a glimpse of the truth but then quickly have to do a rewrite and put her spin on it. Dr Tom realised that and never talked about what the outcome might be; instead he asked her, 'What do you want to do, Annie? I don't mean about treatment, I mean what is the thing that is most important to you, in your life, at this moment?'

She told him she wanted to finish the book she was writing about Cambodia and to do that she needed to go there again.

'Okay, that's what we'll do,' he said. 'We'll get you to Cambodia.'

Travelling and writing was her thing. A strange kind of traveller, in that she would travel armed with irritation, ever ready to be disappointed and aggravated, but that was her unique kind of openness and humour. I remember her being as excited to visit the city of Preston as she had been to visit the ancient lost city of Petra in Jordan. How often have I listened to someone banging on about their world travels and thought, 'Well, it's not made you any more interesting, has it? No, please don't show me photos. I can already grasp how boring you are. Oh no, the phone's coming out. I may have to start self-harming.' Annie could make a trip to the supermarket into a story that made you sorry you weren't there. Adventures could happen anywhere. Enter Annie swearing and dropping things . . . seeing the world and getting annoyed.

If I was a psychiatrist, which I'm not – 'Oh, aren't you, Jo?' 'No.' – I might say it started with her first trip abroad, aged four and a half, when our parents moved from Northern Ireland to the mainland.

She'd been living very happily by the seaside in Newcastle, County Down, and was uprooted to RAF Sealand, right on the Welsh–English border, when my dad joined the RAF. She wrote about it in her book *Irish Blood, English Heart, Ulster Fry*, which was published by Penguin in 2005. I can hear her voice so strongly in this excerpt, her dramatic, bossy little self.

> I was four when we moved from Northern Ireland. I was too young to think anything much about leaving, but England was a disappointment. For one thing, talk of England had all been a trick, because we seemed to be in Wales.

James, Mum, Granny, me and Annie at my grandparents'
in County Tyrone. Summer holidays – can't you tell
from our clothes?

Geography was one of many weak areas in my head when I was four years old, but I could tell the words weren't the same: England, Wales. So they needn't think I was fooled.

I'd been hopeful of England because I had worked out that England was where cartoons happened. I knew cartoons didn't happen in Northern Ireland, I could see that looking out the window, so I was sure that they must happen in that other place, the only other place I'd heard of, England.

England would be bright coloured, teeming with talking bears, rabbits and exploding cats. Looking out of the window in England would be as good as watching television.

But North Wales looked like Northern Ireland. And cartoons, my father informed me, as I wept on our new kitchen floor, happened in a place that 'wasn't real'. Whatever that meant. Not only had we pitched up in a profoundly disappointing place, I had to start school among unintelligible children and learn songs in a whole new language. Songs about birds sitting on the roof of a house. To this day I know the Welsh for 'the bird is on the roof of the house'. I can't say it's stood me in good stead.

My interest in the place rallied when new neighbours moved on to the base. Black Americans. I immediately started stalking them.

Despite me, the new neighbours became very friendly with my mother. My mother and I started using American words for things – *candies, the movies, the trunk of the car* . . . The Americans gleefully copied my mother's reverse Irish/English: 'Would you not have a cup of tea?' We were always calling in and out of each other's houses, swapping dishes of food and not behaving like the other officers' politely boxed-in families.

Too soon, the Americans were posted away. This was worse than the whole trick about cartoons. Something of a drama queen as a child, I was again disappointed to learn that lying on the kitchen floor and weeping loudly didn't change the harsh realities of life.

I persisted with the floor tantrums anyway, just to have something to do now the Americans were gone. Close to the moment when I was going to drive her to have her own floor tantrums, my mother had a reprieve. We had replacement neighbours. New Americans. We were heading round with home-baked soda bread and welcomes right away . . .

I baulked at the sight of them and howled with rage. My mother had lied. These weren't real Americans. They were putting on the accent but I could do that. Did they think I wouldn't notice they were the wrong colour?

As she apologised to the shocked couple from Texas and hauled me wailing home to bed, my mother told me that most Americans were white. I couldn't understand why she was siding with the new neighbours in the plot against me. But there it was, leaving Northern Ireland meant your father started raving about things being 'not real' and your own mother turned against you.

Annie was the first person in our family to go abroad. My parents had never been abroad. My mum said they were abroad already; they were in England, not Northern Ireland. My grandfather had only been abroad because he'd been in the Battle of the Somme in the First World War; he lost half his leg and was poisoned by mustard gas. Maybe that's what put them all off.

So that was the plan: to get better and go to Cambodia. She was writing a book about a woman she'd met there, Sophea. It was to be called *My Cambodian Twin*. Sophea was a classical dancer who had lived through the horrors of the Khmer Rouge regime. Dancers were enemies of the state and many had been executed. Sophea was trying to keep the dance form alive by teaching it to children, but what I think Annie liked most about Sophea was that she was an unlikely heroine, a very irritable Buddhist who made her laugh.

In March 2015, they started her on a course of chemo, but she was too weak. She collapsed – in Peter Jones, of all places. 'Made a right show of myself in the bedding department,' she said.

I think that must have been terrifying, the doctors stopping the chemo. If you can't have the treatments, you can't get better.

But when James and I went to visit her in hospital she was all chat and fun. A hospital very quickly becomes like a village, a village where you're making your home, marking your territory, forming relationships. There was an elderly man there who seemed like an old colonel, she said; he was so dignified and uncomplaining, so grateful and polite to all the staff. She had found her role model in the village; she was going to be like him, a staff favourite. That's Annie's funny ego. She couldn't be just another patient – who wants that? She would be the best patient.

It's a common trait that people try to take charge of their illness. The illness is not them. They don't want pity. No one wants to be pitied, or to have people judging their situation. Also, if you see pity in someone's eyes, maybe it means they are not foreseeing a positive outcome.

And it was *her* cancer. I think that is the best piece of advice I can give you if someone you love gets cancer: just remember, it is *their* cancer. Let them react to it in their own way. Follow their lead. I never read anything about cancer. I just got all my information from her. This did mean that I was completely ignorant of the facts, but that was no bad thing for either of us. If she said she was having the special chemo where you didn't lose your hair, I believed her. What would be the point of saying that Shirley Jones was an actress and not really David Cassidy's mother?

There wasn't much I could do for her, given that I've had absolutely no medical training, but sending money was something I could do. To some people it may not be a worry, but to someone like my sister, who was self-employed, of course money was needed. My advice would be don't ask: they may say no. Think of reasons to send money, like a birthday or buying clothes to cheer themselves up. Get their BACs details and just send some money every now and again, but don't make a big deal out of it. I would sometimes put money in Annie's account and just say I had sent some 'no worry money'.

Send cards as well, but not get-well-soon cards; when someone has cancer a get-well-soon card just seems ludicrously inappropriate – it's cancer, for fuck's sake. I would just try to find cards that would make her and Martin laugh. I remember I found one that had a picture of a rabbit reading a copy of *Watership Down*; inside, it had the same rabbit clutching the book and saying 'WTF!' It's hard to find the right cards, but weirdly that was a good one. It made her laugh.

Annie had to get strong enough to have chemo, and it was Martin's job to fatten her up. Such simple basic creatures we are. With all the advances of modern medicine, the best way for Dr Tom to see that she was improving was if she was eating and putting on weight.

Martin and his (in Annie's view) peculiar relationship with food had been something we had joked about many times before she was ill. She thought it very odd that Martin ate three, sometimes four, meals a day – I know, like a normal human being. She'd say, 'Martin talks about our meals and plans them.' I know, again, like a normal human being. But Annie thought it was 'excessive'. Food was fuel. She would happily have eaten the same meal every day. She put it down to him being six foot five. 'If he wasn't so tall, I'd think he was eating just to annoy me.' But now it turned out to be a great bonus that she was living with a 'feeder'.

I was still in the middle of my stand-up tour, travelling all over the country. So I just sent her emails from everywhere I went in the hope of keeping her entertained and making her laugh.

I travel on my own. I don't have 'people' – there's no driver, tour manager or support act. I don't have the budget for that. It's just me – I am the show. I was now seeing the downside of having moved from London to Edinburgh. If you're doing a show in Exeter, you don't want to be starting your trip in Edinburgh.

Fortunately, however, I love doing the shows, I love being a comedian and I get paid for doing things that in most jobs would get you fired: making smart-arse remarks, messing around, insulting people and encouraging them to ditch their responsibilities. I'm also allowed to drink at work and I get a round of applause just for showing up (and it's not a sarcastic round of applause like your boss might give you . . . at least I don't think it is).

Travelling was a good thing to chat about. It got Annie talking about her own travels and herself – and who doesn't like talking about themselves? We talked about how being a woman on your own makes other people uncomfortable, particularly staying in hotels. During the week it's all right – 'That lone woman is here on business' – but a lone woman in a hotel at the weekend is a freak who shouldn't be there and is spoiling things for 'normal' people. Sunday morning breakfast is where they really punish you. I remember one hotel on the tour where I was seated at a huge table in the corner of the room far away from everyone else, as though I had to be quarantined.

The waitress had seemed confused by my solitary presence, asking me three times, 'Is yourself being joined by someone else?' I was confused at being referred to as 'yourself' – when did people start doing that? It made it sound like it wasn't me she was asking about. But when she finally realised 'yourself' was on her own she clearly thought the only solution to 'the problem' was to corral me in a corner and give me a look that said, 'Now, no biting the happy couples.' Then she added, 'If yourself needs anything from myself or myself's colleagues, just ask and we'll help yourself.' I couldn't help it, I had to ask: 'Is the buffet help yourself?'

Although Annie's travelling was a lot more challenging and adventurous than my Premier Inn outside Chippenham.

Annie planning her next adventure in
County Down.

5

An RAF Childhood,
Ribena and Sherry

Squadron Leader William Caulfield.

I was actually very excited to be in Chippenham because we'd lived on an RAF base near there when I was about four. It was where I'd seen Santa and his reindeers. My dad was an English teacher but had joined the Air Force in 1961. 'Was your dad a pilot? Did he fly planes?' people ask excitedly when they hear he was in the Air Force. No, he didn't. Very few people are actually pilots: pilots are the glamorous elite. My dad worked for the Education Corp. He was responsible for continuing people's education, getting them through O- and A-levels, and preparing them for a return to civilian life – suggesting jobs or retraining. In the mid-seventies his job changed, and officers from Saudi Arabia, Bahrain, Cyprus and other alien places turned up in our living room. My dad was to teach them English but also the subtleties of British life and etiquette. He did this by getting them drunk and starting singalongs with his ukulele. My mother would hand out snacks and explain who George Formby was. The meaning of 'When I'm cleaning windows' was confusing and did not set a good example – it's basically a song about a pervert. One night, when there had been one too many lessons in gin drinking, Colonel Abdullah pulled out a knife and went for a small Greek captain. My dad told us about it over breakfast. He was laughing, but he said it had been touch-and-go: the not-so-ceremonial knife was nearly at the captain's throat. My dad had burst into a calming rendition of 'Danny Boy' and that seemed to distract everyone. My dad is the least likely person to sing 'Danny Boy', but George Formby clearly got everyone far too excited. For a while, a family from Saudi Arabia lived opposite us and they would regularly bring round delicious dishes of food as gifts. This then put a lot of pressure on my mum to make a return visit with a delicious dish of food; at one point she was cooking more for the Rasheed family than she was for us. 'You're having brown bread and sausages. The pie is for Mrs Rasheed.'

Air Force bases are like huge villages that have lots of houses but no shops or pubs and all the houses are built in the same style, like a sort of feudal estate. They were usually in remote locations and weren't served by local buses as no one was meant to know we were there: we were a secret from the Russians. Accommodation was split into two different quarters: one

RAF Newton, Nottinghamshire, 1974. Red brick,
metal windows and flared jeans that don't fit.

for officers and their families and one for airmen and their
families. They were always positioned on opposite sides of the
camp. I remember a friend from primary school who was an
airman's daughter. She was playing in our garden, and it was
one of those long summer evenings so we were out quite late.
When her dad came to get her, I saw him standing on the
roadside waving over the fence, then he came round to the
back door. He saluted my dad and called him sir. I didn't like
that. I instinctively worried how that would make my friend
feel about me. My dad liked it, though; he made some remark
about that being the way one should behave, how an airman
shouldn't come to the front door. He said something about
him being a very decent person, something nice, but even aged
seven I felt there was something wrong with it. I thought it was
demeaning for my friend's dad, even though I wouldn't have
known what demeaning meant. I just knew it wasn't right that
he felt he had to go to the back door.

It seemed silly, like my mum having women round for 'coffee mornings' and 'sherry mornings'. Well, they weren't women; they were 'wives'. That's how they were referred to. The 'wives', unlike my mum, didn't work, they were just 'officers' wives'. My mum would look beautiful and be referred to as Margaret by the wives whereas my dad always called her Maggie. My mum could do a good Margaret. She'd put on her more English 'coffee morning voice', a voice she still puts on when she answers the phone. Most importantly for Annie, James and me, there would be cake left behind. We knew that the sherry drinkers would eat the cake so the coffee mornings were our favourites. I can't think of anything worse than drinking sherry in the morning with no food. Clearly they all got hammered and were desperate to soak up the sherry with cake – officers' wives made into human trifles.

I used to do an impression of the sherry mornings, which unsurprisingly were much noisier than the coffee mornings. It was probably my first observational routine. Mum asked me to do the impression for my dad. I just hooted with a high-pitched laugh and then copied the station commander's wife, saying in a very posh voice, 'Oh, Margaret, it was amazing! I saw a pig! A *pig*!' And then I'd laugh like a maniac and wobble my hair about and say, 'Oh, Margaret, my hair! My hair's falling off!'

The station commander's wife wore wigs, different wigs, so there was no pretence that it was her real hair. It was just different hair wobbling about on her head like a live, hairy hat. My parents would get me to do the impression for selected friends. Annie told me that I mustn't ever do the impression in front of the station commander's wife, but she said it in such a way that I knew the ultimate challenge was to do it in front of her. I think her name was Dotty or Dolly or something very sixties. I can still feel the terror of Annie asking Dotty or Dolly if she would like to hear my impressions. My mum glared at me. Oh my God! Complete panic, then the bread man. Phew. I did an impression of the bread man who came round the camp. Not my best. Well, he was a very old man from Norfolk and I was a seven-year-old girl.

I tried to get onto the base near Chippenham to take a photo of our old house, but it's now an army base and they were very snippy and clearly thought I was suspicious. A security van waved me over to the side of the road and, I'll be honest, I almost shat myself – visions of them thinking I had a gun, wrestling me to the ground and shooting me in the head.

As a family we all unanimously agree that that house near Chippenham was the most beautiful house we ever lived in. We never lived in a house like that again. A huge house in Cotswold stone, with a massive garden, it had been built after the First World War when the Air Force was in its infancy. It had a pantry, an Aga and a strange annexe off the kitchen called the Batman's Room.

Disappointingly, this was not where Bruce Wayne would emerge from to fight crime in Gotham City, although its original purpose was equally bizarre. It was where an officer's manservant, the batman, would sit and polish shoes and shine uniform buttons and do whatever other valet-like jobs an officer needed doing back then. Brasso is a Proustian smell from my childhood, that and the greeny-purple-copper-coloured stains on the remnants of old sheets that my dad used to polish the metal buttons on his uniform (he had to do it himself – in the late sixties only the highest ranks still had batmen). We used the batman's room

33

as a playroom. Which sounds very grand. And it was. But it was just the luck of the draw when they allocated housing to a newly posted family. This big fancy house was empty so we got it. The playroom was a place we were allowed to destroy, but more importantly for my mum, it was impossible to sneak out of there without her noticing. The room was comfortingly messy. Watercolour paints in metal boxes, crayons, coloured pencils, colouring books, spirograph sets and reams of plain paper – such a shame none of us was remotely artistic. We were all quite ham-fisted and barely able to even colour within the lines.

Naturally, Annie was in charge of all games and activities. Once, she told me to drink a cup of Ribena. I did. It was purple paint. I suppose the game was that I would mime drinking the coloured water like we did in our dolls' tea parties but the dolls were smarter than me. I must have assumed that my older sister had sort of messianic powers and could turn water into Ribena so I drank the lot. Annie was shocked. 'Why did you drink paint water? You wouldn't eat mud pies, would you?'

I made a note never to try and eat mud pies again.

There were bells in each room of the house and a display in the kitchen that told the servants which room you were in so they could come when you rang. (No, we didn't have serv-ants.) I don't know what servants people had when the houses were built in the twenties; maybe even then it was just to make people feel that they were the sort of people who could have servants, but didn't.

The garden had all sorts of different areas for playing in. I often played *Pogle's Wood* in the sand pit. *Pogle's Wood* was my favourite TV show. As the name says, it was set in a wood, so I don't know why I played in the sandpit, but childhood games were a lot like dreams – you didn't question the odd logic or who could appear in them. The game was that I lived in the sandpit and Annie would come and visit me with some shopping.

'Hello, Mrs Sandpit. Here's some twigs from the shops in *Pogle's Wood*.' Then Annie would go off and I would stay in the sandpit and quite happily sort out my twigs. It's funny, but if you told me to do that now I would still enjoy sorting twigs and playing house. We don't change that much.

I was a very domesticated child. Loved wearing a pinny
and hanging my dolls' clothes on the line.

★

After Wiltshire we got posted to North London, to a small fifties red-brick terraced house. The change of venue didn't affect me at all – I had no feelings of being uprooted or of missing the big house – but Annie was heartbroken. She would swoon about mournfully like some Jane Austen heroine who had 'come down in the world'. She repeatedly told me that she thought it was all just a terrible dream, that we would wake up and we wouldn't be in Hendon; we'd be back in Wiltshire. Back in the life she was meant to have, in the big house with the big garden and the possibility of servants.

Hendon ended up being her favourite place. She loved Colindale Primary School, loved all the different kinds of friends she had – London children, not RAF children. RAF children were all the same; we all had the same not-from-any-where accent and the same kind of life. When I was in Berlin a few years ago I went to the DDR Museum, where they showed you what life was like in East Germany under communism. It seemed strangely familiar, then I realised it was like growing up in the forces in the seventies. We all had the same regula-tion magnolia walls in our homes, we all knew where our dads worked and who they worked for, and we all knew there was an enemy – the enemy was actually the people in the photographs in the DDR Museum. This was at the height of the Cold War.

Annie, James and I were never materialistic as adults and I wonder if that's why. No one talked about 'stuff' when we were growing up, because all the families had the same 'stuff' – regu-lation forces furniture, solid G-Plan-like, in heavy plain wood (the only variation being the stain of the thick varnish – light or dark). By the age of five I had already moved house four times, but the bed I slept in, although it wasn't my bed, was exactly the same as the bed in the previous house. The same dependable, heavy wood furniture.

The kids in Colindale Primary were different; some had cockney accents and were called Donna or Tracey or Wayne. Donna was my favourite name. Donna had a flared trouser suit and seemed eighteen rather than six. Richard and Joseph in my class were black. Some kids were Asian or Jewish. Up until then the most diverse people we'd met were our Irish parents. I remember Annie telling me that Ruth Garden was Jewish, how excited we both were by this. I had no idea what it meant. I pictured Ruth from my children's Technicolor Bible stories, who was pretty with long dark shiny hair and stood in a wheat field. She did something good and holy, but I wasn't sure what (Ruth in the children's Bible, not Ruth in Colindale Primary). I've since looked her up, and Ruth in the Bible is not actually of the Hebrew tribe; her claim to fame was that when her husband died she stayed and looked after her mother-in-law like a dutiful daughter. Poor Ruth, it wasn't much of a life: you're heartbroken by the death of your husband and then you have to devote the rest of your life to his mother.

Fuck that. Although it does make me think we can't just blame men for writing the Bible; it was clearly men who were in thrall to their mothers.

★

My best friend at Colindale was Jean, a non-RAF child. I was very envious of Jean. She called her mother 'Mum', not 'Mummy', and lived in a thirties mock-Tudor terraced house on the same road as our school and her dad wore a boiler suit when he came home from work. These were all things I found fascinating. Plus, the dad in the boiler suit was very handsome and may have started my lifelong attraction to men who are not middle-class. One Christmas, Jean asked for an Etch A Sketch and got an Etch A Sketch; I also asked for an Etch A Sketch and got a set of oil paints and an easel. I was six. Other people's children always seemed to get the presents they asked for at Christmas, whereas we got the educational alternative. Annie reminded me that when I was eight, I asked for a blackboard, a little one with chalks; instead I was given a typewriter and a Pitman *Teach Yourself Touch Typing* book. (Which, with hindsight, was a great gift and would have been very useful in my itinerant future if I'd actually used it and learned how to touch type.)

RAF Hendon has long ceased to be a working base; in fact part of it is now the Royal Air Force Museum. The place you used to live in being a museum doesn't half make you feel old. There are still other relics in the area that show it was there, like a street sign for Aerodrome Road. In the late sixties it was a huge area of hangars and runways and still had bomb-damaged buildings from the Second World War. A brilliant place for kids to play, unsupervised, as kids were then. Any accidents were dealt with later with iodine or a tetanus shot depending on the severity of the 'play'.

That some of our favourite places to play were air raid shelters makes my childhood seem to be from such a different era. From the outside they are large grassy mounds which are great for rolling down; on the top was the entrance, with a hatch like a submarine. Nowadays these would, of course, be safely blocked off and sealed for ever with metal plates and *Danger Keep Out* notices. But back then adults weren't very concerned with children's safety – they weren't very concerned with children at all, really. You could climb down inside the shelter and scream a lot. That's all I remember happening. Annie or James would go first, then one of them would say they saw a rat or something moving in the darkness and we would all scream and scramble back up the ladder. We would then have to do some therapeutic rolling down the mound to calm ourselves after all the screaming.

Happy days.

6

Chelsea Pensioners and Cancer Hats

The effects of the chemo were starting to take their toll. Maybe there is not enough warning about what the treatments are really like. The cancer charity adverts show people joking around while having their chemo; they don't show them at home afterwards vomiting and feeling too weak to speak. Annie hadn't been prepared for how bad she would feel, or maybe she'd just been telling herself it was all going to be fine. Until it wasn't.

I got this email.

From: Annie Caulfield
To: Jo Caulfield
Sent: 26 March 2015
Subject: Meeting

All good so far, it's the weekend the crap might hit but I won't be so scared if it does. But it won't.

Monday should be good. We could have a potter to the Chelsea Pensioners' garden and new tearooms. Pretty garden, small to walk round and old people don't have many germs. What time do you think? Martin can alert if bad things happen but I'm feeling v. optimistic.

One crap thing Dear – the 'your hair is unlikely to fall out' thing? Bullshit. Down to nearly nothing in a week. So went out with M the length of Kings Road to find head gear that isn't turban-y or that obvious headscarf of cancer thing. It will grow back in a couple of months so it's just a temporary horribleness. And marvellous Macmillan can get you free designer wigs. I have a couple on order although I'm not sure about that ... Woodrow is also going hat shopping for me as he feels that's what he can do well ... I'm going to end up with a hat collection and taking naps ... OMG! I've turned into Father.

So Monday, with me wearing God knows what on my head, just let me know what time. Probably easiest if you collect me at flat and we wander over to Pensioners' gardens? x

I know in the grand scheme of things losing your hair for a bit isn't the worst thing in the world, blah, blah, blah, but it doesn't exactly help your mood. It really is adding insult to injury. What could make them feel worse at this time?

'They could grow a beard or get spots . . . No, I've got it, all their hair could fall out!' 'Perfect.' What a bastard thing to happen.

There was no proudly sporting a bald head like you see in cancer dramas with Annie. She didn't want to advertise to strangers that she had cancer. She was always on the lookout for caps and hats that didn't look like 'cancer hats', as she called them.

Annie was strangely ashamed of having cancer. I think it made her feel almost unbearably vulnerable. She didn't want anyone but a small close circle to know. She didn't want people picking over her cancer, delving into it. Those of us who had been told were to tread very carefully, but not so carefully as to be fussy and annoying. Yeah, it was tricky.

I understood Annie not wanting people to know. She was always a private person, always had a protective coating. People who didn't know her would just see this very eloquent, funny and intelligent woman, but if you knew her, you would see the vulnerability – the little girl who hadn't got over something.

Throughout our lives my brother and I have had to tread carefully. We'd say the wrong thing but not know it was the wrong thing. She would lash out, not because she was mean, but because she was hurt. Like you'd flicked salt on an open wound but you had no idea the wound was there or what caused it.

She had her little group now: as well as Martin, James and me, there were her friends Woodrow and Sarah. Woodrow was good for fun 'perking-up' visits, she said. He's a geeky cartoon-ist with a slightly autistic unemotional personality (and I say that with great affection, Woodrow). She could be pretty sure he wouldn't ask anything too personal; he would just bring silly books and comics to entertain her. Woodrow was also the only person who Annie would allow to 'pop in'. She was very much against the random caller, but with Woodrow it was fine, some-how part of his charm. 'I can't stop him. He doesn't understand normal hours – he'll just come in through the window any time of day or night.' Annie was interested in graphic novels and animation; I think they might've collaborated on a cartoon at one point. It was another way of writing so she wanted to know about it.

At this point I'd never met Sarah, but I'd heard about her for years. Annie was always full of stories about Sarah and her 'merry band of drunk, marauding lesbians'. They seemed to be constantly disgracing themselves and not giving a shit. I don't know if the 'marauding' and being gay had anything to do with each other, I am just reporting, so no offence to any lesbians, marauding or otherwise. Sarah was a writer too, a writer Annie admired; it's unusual amongst writers to have a friendship with no envy or jealousy, but they did. Sarah is a couple of years older than Annie and had pushed the boundaries: she was one of the first women writers to have a play on at the National Theatre. They met when they were both on a writing team for a soap opera on the BBC World Service. Annie liked Sarah's extrovert nature and raucous sense of humour. Also, that she didn't wear her intelligence like a big boring scarf to choke the life out of a room. Annie always hated pomposity in writers.

Sarah had sadly lost her partner to ovarian cancer six years previously. She said that something good had come out of that awfulness – she might be able to help Annie with things she had learned while nursing her partner. Sarah was full of good ideas and advice and (much to her surprise) Annie took her advice as gospel. She needed to have people to share this with like Sarah and Dr Tom. Carefully chosen people, not everyone, just a few, as though she'd wrapped up the cancer in little parcels, and then carefully given it out so she didn't have to carry it all herself. (Parcels of cancer? Note to self: maybe steer clear of analogies.)

Annie was someone who didn't trust people easily, so to be given her trust was – and I'm nearly going parcels again – something very special. All her friends knew that.

★

Annie was on good form when I took her out to the Chelsea Pensioners. We had cake, and she walked all the way there and back. She lived nearby. I know. La-di-da. How fancy pants. But before you get thinking we are old-money posh people, she lived in a Peabody housing association flat. She'd been there since the late eighties. It was a small flat, but in the most beautiful location and at a controlled, reasonable rent. She'd qualified for the flat in 1988 because she was a writer; back then Peabody were helping artists with accommodation and encouraging them to live in the city. Now, they're given to key workers – nurses, teachers and so on. In the eighties a teacher could easily afford to live in London – what a different time. Now half the private homes nearby are left empty, owned by oligarchs who have bought them to park their money in the UK. Even regular old-money posh people who used to live in Chelsea have been priced out. The sort of ladies in tweeds who used to come up from their country house and charge about Peter Jones looking for comfortable shoes and hats for 'Jocasta's wedding'. Annie always liked them; they had the politeness and decency of posh people in British war films like *Mrs. Miniver* (look it up, lovely film).

The Chelsea Pensioners' Hospital is a beautiful building, with grounds you can walk in and a nice café, plus, of course, lots of Chelsea Pensioners bobbling about for a bit of colour. They look sweet and *Dad's Army*-ish but they've all been soldiers. We used to think about where and when they had served, how some of them might've been right hard bastards in their day, trained killers, and now they all look cute and wave at you. Margaret Thatcher's ashes are buried in the grounds and Annie took me to see her grave. She said we had to act like we liked her or they wouldn't let us in. I hoped it was obvious just by looking at us that we weren't people who liked Margaret Thatcher.

Martin had told me that the wigs she'd ordered had arrived a few days ago and they'd been thrown across the room in a temper and not mentioned again. When I brought her back to the flat after our outing I saw one, abandoned, sitting on the floor under the radiator like a dead cat. She had sent away for them so full of hope. I don't quite know what a 'fright wig' is, but that's what this looked like – nothing remotely like Annie's hair (or anyone's hair). It was something more suited to Harpo Marx. It was sad to think of Annie putting it on and being disappointed, looking at herself in the mirror and seeing this flattened guinea pig perched on her head. It made me cry. It would have been such a big thing if the wig had worked out.

I was finding it all very difficult but not in the way one thinks these things will be difficult. I was stretched in different ways. Still on the road four days a week on tour, on my free days I wanted to go to London to see Annie and then to Edinburgh to be at home with my husband. Also, we were selling our flat in Edinburgh. It was a beautiful flat near the Meadows area, with big rooms and high ceilings, and huge sash-and-case windows. But while living there I had learned what people in Scotland meant when they talked about a tenement having 'a good stair'. These big sandstone buildings were purpose-built as apartments between around 1880 and 1920. Each block has a big main door, and all the flats share a main staircase. To have 'a good stair' means you have good neighbours: ones who share sweeping the landings and don't slam the heavy main door or make a racket when they come in and out. A considerate stair. Ours was a tale of 'when good stairs turn bad'; it only took two flats changing hands for it to all change. Loud posh students banging up and down the stair all day and night. We'd also got tired of the area. I'd fallen in love with Leith; the mix of people there suited me better than Morningside. It's the old dockside area of the city. There's always something going on at a bus stop in Leith, always someone up to something, yet people are considerate and there's a real sense of community.

One night, in the Central Bar at the foot of the Walk – a place with fantastic Victorian tiling and lots of older guys who look like they might have boxed a bit in their youth and where sometimes they have singers, middle-aged women belting out country and western with the authenticity of having lived a tough life – one of the older guys leaned in to me and said, 'You know, you're the best-looking woman in here.' He then turned and glanced round the bar and added, 'I know that's no' saying much, mind.' A truly Scottish compliment.

At the same time as all this, my mum was telling me that my dad wasn't well. My parents still didn't know that Annie had cancer, and I was mad at them, angry and resentful with them for something they didn't even know about. I felt constantly guilty about not being there enough for my mum.

It's another reason Annie didn't want to tell our parents: she was frightened of my dad's reaction. It's not that he would have wanted Annie to be ill, but he was excited by illness. It was his hobby. He'd been sickly in a vague way for years. Ever since he'd taken early retirement he seemed to have devoted himself to seeing how many times he could get the local GPs to make house calls. Nothing was ever officially diagnosed; he'd be fine for weeks and then he'd start diagnosing himself with illnesses and take to his bed. And cancer, well, that's the big one, that would've been like hitting the jackpot to my dad. He would have googled himself into a frenzy of amateur prognoses and treatments, which he wouldn't have kept to himself. He would've excitedly told Annie all about his findings.

That's what she was scared of: my dad intruding into her

life and making her feel bad. Something my dad had always been able to do, whether he meant to or not. My mum said he was proud of her but he had a way of showing off about her achievements that Annie found both mortifying and undermining. I've seen it in other families, the proud parent who messes up and no one quite understands what everyone's done wrong. Why can't we just say what we mean and get on? Because then families would be too simple.

Another person she hadn't told about having cancer was her oldest friend, Molly. Molly was her best friend from school, they had had years of adventures together and Annie was god-mother to Molly's daughter, Jazz. I think Annie was trying to protect Molly, and protect herself, too. Molly's brother, Patrick, a huge, larger-than-life character who Annie had loved dearly, had died from a brain tumour fifteen years earlier. Telling Molly would bring up Patrick. Patrick had died, but she wasn't going to die. This was not to be associated with Patrick.

Annie had built all this up in her head, imagining all sorts of reactions, reactions that might be difficult. I do the same thing, creating huge dramas in my head till I drive myself nuts and say, 'Oh God, just do it!'

She waited till she was coming to the end of her radio-therapy, when she was feeling strong and hopeful. When she did tell Molly, Molly, in a perfectly normal way, was emotional. I know Molly meant no harm. She was genuinely sad because she loves Annie, but she had broken the unspoken rule: Annie mustn't see anyone upset. We were all pretending there was nothing to be upset about. I, of course, genuinely thought there was nothing to be upset about. I was living in happy ignorance, believing what Annie told me.

7

Nuns, T. Rex and
Other Impure Thoughts

Going back to boarding school. Annie is wearing her
bottle-green Sunday suit. I wore that same tunic from the
age of eight till I left at fourteen. You can tell by the huge hem.

Annie and I had gone to boarding school – that's where she and
Molly met. Lots of the pupils were, like us, 'Forces children',
with their school fees paid by the Ministry of Defence. There

were postings all over the world and you got posted every two to three years so you had to change schools every time. That was the reason given for boarding children but would changing schools have been so bad? I had already been to three schools and hadn't found it at all traumatic.

I know there is an assumption that boarding school means you are posh and rich. My parents weren't rich but, if they were to answer honestly, they did aspire to be considered posh. Julie Tiernan's parents *were* rich. She was probably the only genuinely rich person at the school. Her dad had a Rolls-Royce but was very much not posh; he came from County Mayo and 'made his money in building'. I must have overheard that – it just rings with seventies prejudice.

Annie went to boarding school when she was eleven. I went three weeks before my ninth birthday. Maybe I would have been just as homesick if I'd gone at eleven, but I think it affected me more because I was so young. I just didn't understand why my parents had sent me away. What had I done to make them send me away? But to my parents this was a great opportunity. They got to send their children to boarding school: we would be middle-class and well educated.

Being middle-class was important to my dad, which is maybe why he often tried a little too hard. The fact that he went through a phase of wearing a monocle should give you an idea. His joining the RAF as an officer meant that we could pass for middle-class/upper-middle-class. Success. It was as though my dad turned himself into the grown-up version of posh people he'd read about in books or heard on the wireless as a child in Belfast. He was really too unconventional and flamboyant to be in the Air Force. He wanted to be David Niven in Second

World War RAF films, not to actually be in the RAF where he didn't get to fly planes and everyone was very conservative and liked obeying rules.

Presentation Convent, Matlock, Derbyshire. Ever the drama queen, Annie is the one in the middle falling back on everyone.

★

The boarding school we went to was in fact a convent. It was such a weird place; it was as if we were at school in the nineteen-forties. For example, we had to wear two pairs of pants: first, our 'civilian' coloured pants, but then, over those we had to wear heavy pants made of thick sweatshirt material that came up to your waist – 'interlocking knickers', the nuns called them. And, just to make sure there was no semblance of femininity knicker-wise, they were shit-brown in colour.

Annie was known as Tom when she was at school. She was a big personality and always seemed to be causing some sort of controversy or minor rebellion, acts that in no way seem rebellious now, like when she played T. Rex in assembly. That had been hugely shocking. Each week there was a 'modern' assembly and you were allowed to play a record. It was usually something by Peter, Paul and Mary or Simon & Garfunkel (the nuns loved a bit of 'Bridge Over Troubled Water'). Annie played 'Jeepster' by T. Rex. Four minutes and nine seconds of sexy guitar and lyrics about people being 'jeepsters' for love. It also has the line: 'You've got the universe reclining in your hair.' What a great line. Who could object to that? Nuns, apparently. A nod from headmistress Sister Gabriel and three nuns scurried over to the record player. They then hovered over it, whispering worriedly. Sister Mary was nominated and she delicately lifted the arm up and away from the record, with all the care and precision of a bomb disposal expert.

Molly and 'Tom' were best friends, but even that broke the rules. Molly was a 'day girl', and there was some unwritten rule that boarders weren't meant to be friends with day girls. I don't know if it was a snobby thing, or if it was because they went home at night and at the weekends, so would be a pretty useless friend because they weren't there most of the time. Or maybe we would become so charged with jealousy because they got to go home and be with their parents that it would make friendship impossible; they'd not been through it, they weren't battle-scarred boarders.

Annie was constantly arguing with the nuns. She stopped believing in God (and also in wearing two pairs of pants) as soon as she hit puberty. I wasn't consciously rebellious, but I always seemed to be in trouble anyway – 'unbridled' was how one nun described me in a school report. Like an untamed horse? Quite a nice thing to be, I think.

The snapshot in my head is of Annie and Molly laughing, always laughing. I was still very much a child when they were in sixth form. The sixth formers seemed like adults. Looking back at old school photos they still seem like adults. There's something about those mid-seventies clothes that meant children went from knee socks and looking like extras in an episode of *Just William* to American Tan tights, A-line skirts and looking like they could totally boss a PTA meeting.

Saturday morning at the convent, 1976. Annie is far right, rocking a pair of platform wedges.

One of my happiest memories was telling my hockey teacher to piss off when I was about thirteen. I still remember the thrill of not caring about the consequences. She blew the whistle and said I had committed a foul, and I just said, 'Oh, piss off.' It felt great, and rather than getting me in trouble they treated me like I'd had some sort of breakdown. I was sent to the nurse, who asked me if I had started my menstrual cycle and then bizarrely gave me some cough medicine. I get the same feeling now when I insult people in the audience at gigs. A fun, free, powerful feeling that there are no consequences, that I know how far I can push it. It's a *great* feeling.

From an early age Annie seemed aware of her image, that you could reinvent yourself, project a different version of yourself to the world. You didn't have to just go along with everything, accept things as they were – no, you had to think bigger. The convent was in Matlock, a small town in Derbyshire, but somehow it was like she was part of the Algonquin Round Table, reading F. Scott Fitzgerald, James Baldwin and Dorothy Parker. And there wasn't a group of girls at the convent who were into that. No, it was just her. She was her own invention.

She was the first girl to win a debate against the local boys' school. All the sixth formers were in the debating society, mainly because every term there was an inter-school debate with the local Jesuit school. That meant contact with boys. It's funny how I can still remember the boys they all swooned over, boys I never saw but whose names had the resonance of Mr Darcy or Heathcliff – Paul De Haviland, Simon O'Shaughnessy, Michael Fitzgerald . . .

Without fail the boys always voted for the boys' team. The girls also voted for the boys' team, either because they were in love with one of the boys or just thought boys were better at everything and that was the way the world was. Annie getting the boys to vote for her was huge. Everyone was talking about it when they came back that night. It was like it wasn't my sister, it was this stranger, 'Tom Caulfield'. Years later Annie said she remembered feeling so happy and excited that she'd won, but then after the debate, the dreamy boys still just went and spoke to the two prettiest girls in the class. Nothing had changed and she realised boys were idiots.

For my first two years at boarding school I was in a different building to Annie. My building was two hundred yards down the hill from the senior school, and on Sundays older sisters were allowed to visit for an hour. That hour was so important. I was so miserable that I would just cling to Annie when it was time for her to go back up the hill.

When I moved up to the senior school I thought I would see more of her, but she was always this fleeting, exciting grown-up. I was less miserable by then, though, so it was okay. Is it always that way? The younger sibling always wanting to be with the older sibling and the older sibling oblivious.

It's strange the times that my brain has chosen to remember. One is being allowed to go with her and her friends when they went for a smoke in the woods and finding a dead fox. It stank, it was covered in maggots and was oddly liquid-looking, so we all wanted to run away screaming. But we couldn't as it might give away the location of the illegal smoking area, so we had to leave casually, one at a time.

Another memory is watching Annie and her roommates pluck their eyebrows; they plucked and plucked until they just had thin arched lines, like they'd all stood too close to a fire in a cartoon. Scorched sophistication. Not quite the Marlene Dietrich cool they were going for. There would be a strange, scratchy, whirring noise coming from Virginia Dyer's transistor radio; apparently it was Radio Luxembourg. I was so happy just sitting on the bed with these glamorous teenagers who smelled of hairspray and make-up.

To get to the music room for singing class you had to walk through the sixth-form common room. We weren't meant to talk to the sixth formers, even if one of them was your sister. I walked past Annie and Molly laughing and making toast. One of the perks of being sixteen at the convent was that you had full use of a toaster (I still don't quite get why sixteen-year-old girls valued making toast so highly). Annie and Molly were having a conversation with Sister Helen about 'impure thoughts' – it was fascinating and mind-boggling. I wasn't quite sure what they were discussing but I knew it was an extremely daring topic. Annie was arguing: 'How could it be a sin if you were asleep? If they were impure *dreams*.' How indeed?

Sister Helen taught French and was very good-looking but always seemed stressed-out and about to cry. Annie told me that her fiancé had been killed in a car crash and that's why she'd become a nun. Years later I repeated that story to some ex-convent friends. It wasn't true at all; Annie had completely made it up. What a shame, it was such a romantic story. Poor Sister Helen.

Just like with the crazy-paving mud story that could have taken us to Africa, I often got into trouble because I tried to copy Annie or repeat things that she had said. I would get completely out of my depth with misinformation. Once, in Religious Education I was asked to read my essay to the class. Annie had been reading Erich von Däniken's *Chariots of the Gods*, the book first published in 1968 and in which the author argues that all religions are based on aliens being mistaken for gods. Basically Jesus was an astronaut and it could be proved by drawings of spaceships in ancient caves. Yeah, it's just as nuts as most religions. Whether Annie believed this or not, I can't remember, but she had told me about it and I then put it through my own eleven-year-old Catholic filter.

'Josephine, you have written a very peculiar answer to the question "What does Jesus mean to me?" Would you read it to the class, please?' said Sister Una.

Of course as soon as I began reading it out loud it all started to fall apart; it somehow didn't sound as cool and grown-up as it had when Annie had said it. I stumbled on. 'Some people say that Jesus was an astronaut and came down from another planet in a spaceship, but I don't think that matters as he still died on the cross and was crucified for our sins.'

The class sat in stunned silence. They looked at me the same way we'd looked at Fatima Miraandez when she told us she wasn't a virgin any more because she'd fallen off a bunk bed during half term.

★

There is now a Presentation Convent Past Pupils Facebook page, and things all kicked off on there when a former pupil wrote an article in the *Daily Mail* about what an awful school it was and how cruel the nuns had been. I immediately emailed Annie about it. I was always looking for things that might perk her up, and I didn't want to keep asking her how she was. I knew she wasn't doing much apart from eating, sleeping and a bit of writing when she had the energy. It seemed incredible to me that people were outraged by someone saying the school was awful. By today's standards it *was* awful.

My memory is that we were regularly hit with whatever was at hand – slippers, riding crops and, a particular favourite, Mason Pearson hairbrushes. I see them occasionally in Boots; they have a large, flat oval back to them that's perfect for whacking ten-year-olds. The other threat that the nuns made sure to remind us about was 'The Communists'. I remember Sister Ursula telling us that the communists were very likely tunnelling under the convent. We all offered up our prayers that night for God to defeat the communists. We didn't question why they would head for Matlock Bath rather than Westminster or Buckingham Palace. We were terrified of these tunnelling communists because if they got in and took over the convent, we would never see our parents again. Of course that's what the nuns told us. So many dangers in life resulted in you 'never seeing your parents again'. As half of us were Forces children, this seemed a very real threat in the mid–seventies. At home on the base we had different alerts for the likelihood of invasion by the Soviet Union. Dad had told us all the plan: if the siren went off, it meant the USSR was attacking us and my mum was to load us in the car and drive to Ireland – and not stop till Dublin.

There were other punishments that seem tame now but at the time were more terrifying than being smacked with a hairbrush or a riding crop. Or maybe they are as terrifying and macabre as they seemed then. If you were caught talking in the bedroom after 'lights out', you would be made to go down to the cellar and stand there on your own in the dark. The cellar was basically a cold room where we kept our outdoor shoes and gym kits. The school had originally been built as a Victorian sanatorium and was a vast Gothic pile that would've been a perfect location for a Hammer House of Horrors film. Standing in the cellar one night – I was always being sent there as it's impossible for me to not talk – I just couldn't take the darkness and the world of unknown noises, wind or cats or ghosts, so I turned the light on. When the nun on guard duty came to send me back to bed she never remarked on the light being on. From then on we all just turned the light on. Had the nuns meant it to be this terrifying ordeal in the dark? Maybe not.

Nevertheless some past pupils on the Facebook page were definitely looking back at the convent through rose-tinted boaters.

Yes, we wore boaters.

8

Vomiting and Being Irish . . . or Not

Going on our summer holidays to Ireland on the Fishguard
to Rosslare ferry, 1970. Annie is beside herself with excitement
in her new, grown-up raincoat and handbag, James and
I in matching anoraks.

To be fair to the nuns, Annie thrived at boarding school, and in
their own way they encouraged intelligence and independence.
I look on the nuns very differently now; they were women
of their time who had very few choices in life. All the nuns
were Irish. Ireland was basically a theocracy back then, and
parts of it had the most miserable poverty. Joining an order was
often the only way out. Become a nun, or either be married
off to some old farmer who was onto his third wife, or stay at
home looking after all your siblings and your ailing parents. I
remember Sister Christina. She had been a missionary in India

and Africa, taught English literature, and she was one of my favourite teachers. She seemed to have had an extremely interesting and fulfilling life. Once, when I was homesick she told me she understood how I felt; when she'd joined the convent at the age of seventeen she'd been sent to India. She didn't see her mother for fifteen years and she never saw her father again, as he died while she was away. Hopefully having God made her feel better about it all. Or maybe she said it to shut me up, spoilt little madam that I was – I would see my parents in three weeks' time and neither of them would be dead. I was living the life of Riley compared to her.

There were lots of fabulously seventies Irish names at our school, Deidres and Brigids and Bernadettes. We were all second-generation Irish, but this was before everyone started being called Saoirse and Gráinne and Aoife – before the new confident Ireland got the last laugh by giving their children Irish names that the Brits had no idea how to spell or pronounce.

A few years ago Annie wrote a series of children's books set in a boarding school called *Katie Milk Solves Crimes and So On . . .* Reading them again, I think I can recognise some of the nuns and the schoolgirls. The blurb says: 'Meet Katie Milk – she's brave, funny and has an active imagination.' It's Annie.

Great importance was placed on your level of Irishness at the convent. Or maybe that was just in my head. I repeatedly told the nuns my parents were Irish in the hope of better treatment. The nuns would talk to me about Clonmel where my grandma was from, and they were softer and kinder when they talked about Ireland.

There was only one *actual* Irish girl in the school, and we were all fascinated by her. Like she was a celebrity. We expected a lot from this girl who was more Irish than any of us could ever dream of being. She was called Fiona Walsh – we all found the name very disappointing, as she didn't sound nearly as Irish as her roommates Siobhan O'Malley and Bernadette Corcoran, who were from Wigan. Fiona stayed for one term and then left; she told her parents she didn't like it at boarding school and they let her go home. What? Again, that didn't seem very Irish. Weren't we all meant to suffer together at school, to be martyrs and offer our unhappy childhoods to Jesus and make our parents happy by never complaining and then win a place in heaven?

I was very envious that both Annie and James were born in Northern Ireland. It seemed so cool to be able to say you were born there. As kids we all felt both Irish and not Irish; when we went to Northern Ireland we would be all excited about our Irishness and our Irish relatives, but then we would be called 'the English cousins'. No confusion there, then. English, very English cousins (although I was actually born in Wales).

But there were little things that we did in our family that very English people who lived on RAF camps didn't do. Other people's mothers didn't have milk bottles lined up on the kitchen windowsill. They gave off a slightly sweet, rancid smell, 'baby sick' we called it. Mum was letting the milk go off so she could use it like buttermilk to make soda bread. Now you can buy soda farls in Tesco, and I bet Waitrose even stocks buttermilk, but nothing so exotic was available in the seventies.

And, of course, as Irish Catholics my parents were not used to celebrating Guy Fawkes Night, or as my mum called him, 'that poor wee man who never actually did anything to any-one'. Mum thought it was just spiteful of the English to punish him when he hadn't succeeded. Like adding insult to injury.

I loved the Northern Irish accent as a kid (I still do), and Annie and I talked about how hearing that accent was always comforting – like home, I suppose. But was it home? After writing about Australia, Jordan, Egypt, Burkina Faso, Italy, Finland, Benin and Zanzibar Annie went back to Northern Ireland to see if it felt like home, and also to enjoy our relatives. They really are people to enjoy – great talkers.

Irish Blood, English Heart, Ulster Fry is the book that came out of her trips there. It's full of funny observations and history – real history and family history – and other things she was told that may or may not have been true (maybe they were things told to English cousins, because English cousins were fun to tell tall tales to).

We spent summers in Northern Ireland in the late sixties and early seventies. We'd go by car ferry and I'd be sick. Whichever route we took – and we tried them all – I'd be sick. The worst was going from Fishguard in Wales to Rosslare one year. The boat was heaving and lurching, people were clinging on to anything they could to stay upright, and Mummy dragged me to the toilets to be sick. It was literally *awash* with sick. I'd never seen adults vomit before. It was astonishing to me that grown men – a priest! – could literally just throw up where they stood, while saying things like, 'Well, I've kept it off my shoes.' There was something satisfying about seeing adults out of control.

My auntie Mary and uncle Jimmy rented a house in Buncrana, Donegal, where we got to play out with the cousins till nearly midnight. It seemed to be magically light for hours – now I know that's because it's so far west and north – and we were allowed to get dirty and just let ourselves go. Maybe that was geographical, too, being so far away from station commanders' wives.

In Donegal with my cousin Eithne, who
says she can see herself staring, green
with envy, at my swimsuit.

There were eight cousins in one family, and it was all fun
and different to how things were at home, although I was also
scared for my life a lot of the time. The cousins were wild and
fearless. There was an interesting dynamic, and I noticed that
Annie wasn't in charge. Cousin Kate was. Annie very happily
took a subordinate role; this seemed a wise decision, as Kate
was pretty amazing and we would surely die if we didn't have
her protection. I would watch Annie watch Kate – there were
surely things to be learned from cousin Kate.

It's funny to read in Annie's book that she had the same
fear and awe of the cousins, the same feeling that we were a
bit 'prissy' compared to them. They seemed to be constantly
throwing themselves into the Atlantic Ocean for 'a wee swim'
with not a care about the freezing temperature or the huge
crashing waves. Joey (that's me) was to be helped a lot. I
felt like Clara in *Heidi* – some delicate child they had to be
careful of.

'Now wee Joey can't climb trees' – that was strange to me as I'd thought of myself as being very much a tree–climbing kind of a child, but this was the big league: another level of tree climbing.

This is from Annie's book *Irish Blood, English Heart, Ulster Fry*.

My parents would sit drinking tea and playing cards with the other adults, paying no attention to pleas that it was raining, or we wanted to watch television – we were driven out to roam the town and beaches with the cousins.

At that time we were living in London so we weren't used to being left to our own devices from dawn to way after dusk. There were only three of us English weaklings, so any opinion we might have about time to go home had little influence. We didn't like it when it was getting dark; we tired quickly and most bizarrely, in the eyes of our independent cousins, we wanted to see our parents.

This most frightening family of cousins were fast-moving natural leaders, with athletic strength and sarcastic wit. Their favourite place was the scrappy fairground on the sea front. The cousins would defend us if fairground children mimicked our English accents. Stones would be thrown, insults screamed and jumpers pulled. But left looking at us when there was no outside threat, the cousins found us very poor specimens.

My parents followed the bombing campaigns of the seventies and eighties on the nightly news. They were sad to see what was happening to Belfast, the city where my dad had grown up, where they had met as students at Queen's University and courted. Cinemas, dance halls and shops: they had memories of everywhere. Everywhere that was now being blown up.

I didn't empathise with what my parents were going through. I didn't understand it. I don't remember being scared as a child when we were on holiday; it had just changed. There were sandbags piled up on the bridges we drove over, and standing behind them were soldiers with guns. My auntie Mary called us back as we headed into Woolworth's in Portadown; we had to wait for her to get searched before we could go in for some pick and mix. Things happened at night. The adults would talk about someone getting stopped on a certain road or about 'trouble in town' but it was always in a chatty tone, like it was nothing for anyone to worry about. My cousins' lives were radically changed, their teenage years completely different to mine, but they also have a rich sense and love of where they are from. I'm not from anywhere.

We stopped going to Northern Ireland for our summer holidays and went down to my grandma's in Tipperary instead, but by the early seventies it wasn't safe for my dad to go so we stopped visiting completely. My mum would go on her own in her autumn half-term break.

Once, my mum and I were at a petrol station in Nottingham, waiting to pay, and the people in front were talking about an IRA bombing that had just happened. My mum took a moment when we were back in the car. I stared at her and thought, 'Why isn't she starting the car?' She just sat there holding on to the steering wheel, then she said, 'Honest to God, I'm ashamed to open my mouth.'

9

Leaving the Convent Behind

Visiting Annie in London. Annie is wearing a gorgeous,
three-piece, pinstripe trouser suit. And, yes, a perm.
I was still at boarding school.

After the convent and before she went to university, Annie spent
about six months in Paris working as a nanny. The family that
the nuns had helped assign her to lived way out in the suburbs. This wasn't the Paris Annie had dreamed of – this was
more like Aylesbury – so she found a new family who lived in
an apartment near the Bastille. *This* was Paris. My mum and I
recently found the letters she wrote home. They're witty and
self-deprecating, but I can also feel how proud she is of herself. This is the person she wanted to be, the life she wanted
to be living.

65

She then moved back to London and got a live-in job at the Griffin pub on Villiers Street, Charing Cross. It's not a pub any more, it's a Five Guys burger place, but I think there's still a bust of a griffin on the roof. This area under the Arches, where Heaven nightclub is now, used to be famous for coin dealers. It was full of little shops selling coins and old war medals. Suddenly coin dealers were a thing I knew about through Annie; they may well have been perfectly respectable boring businessmen, but the way Annie told it, this was one handshake away from the London underworld. They had nicknames like Tony the Greek and Maltese Jonny. To me it was like Annie was living in an episode of *Budgie*.

For those of you born after 1970, *Budgie* was a show about lovable petty criminals. My parents were big fans. There was the menacing but lugubrious Scottish boss played beautifully by Iain Cuthbertson, and Adam Faith played an ex-con odd job man. Yes, it's *Minder* but made in 1971. Adam Faith is someone I feel I should explain to younger readers. He was part of the British rock 'n' roll scene in the sixties, along with Billy Fury and Marty Wilde (yes, Kim Wilde's dad . . . but who's Kim Wilde? This could take some time). He had some big hits, the biggest probably 'What Do You Want?', but my favourite is 'Made You'. Check out sixties British rock 'n' roll — it's better than you think. Adam Faith wore sharp suits in the sixties, and in the seventies he was the epitome of the lovable cockney in fantastic flared denim trouser suits that I would love to wear now. I watched an episode of *Budgie* on Gold recently and sat there open-mouthed. Adam Faith was still cute and funny, but the storyline was about stealing a van full of pornographic magazines by mistake. There were endless scenes of dialogue with the characters standing next to full-frontal photos of women with huge 'knockers', as they called them then, clearly on display. The female characters were divided into two camps: they were either 'dolly birds' who the men wanted to have sex with or 'battle axes' who they didn't. Good old-fashioned family entertainment . . .

I was still at the convent at the time so I couldn't have been more than fourteen years old, but Annie arranged for me to come down and stay with her in the pub instead of going to my parents for one of my visiting weekends. What a little freak I must've been, so naive and inexperienced, a very young fourteen. I clearly remember there being an Australian barman (it was the seventies, so he must have been one of the first of the Aussies to come over here for work) who laughed his head off and took the piss out of me because I said something was 'ever so good'. He did my voice back at me, a posh little girl's voice: *'Oooh, ever so good!'* How rude, I thought, and also was that really my voice? And if it was, was that a bad thing? I made a mental note about people from Australia; I was wary of these loud, confident people. I had never met people like this, relaxed and unself-conscious but possibly quite dim. People who seemed to think nothing of being rude to your face. To this day I think we should be rude behind each other's backs; we're not animals.

Annie took me to two West End shows that weekend: *Side by Side by Sondheim* (which was probably the thing I said was 'ever so good') and a farce called *I Love My Wife*, starring the late and lovely Richard Beckinsale from *Porridge*. I loved him in *Porridge* and couldn't quite believe that the man from television was actually right in front of me. I don't remember anyone else who was in it, but I do remember that there was a bed onstage and I didn't really understand what was going on. I suspect now that the plot must've been about jumping in and out of bed with people and the guy eventually realising that he didn't want to sleep around because he loved his wife. It's typical of that era that a man was considered a hero because he didn't cheat on his wife (or if he did cheat and then went back to his wife, she was supposed to be happy because 'boys will be boys').

Afterwards we went out for dinner and sat outside and had wine, Muscadet. I'd never heard the word 'Muscadet' before. 'We'll have a bottle of Muscadet.' Annie said this was what French people did, and I remember feeling very, very French (or possibly very drunk) and it all seeming fantastic and glamorous. She only had her wages from the pub to live on, and this must have cost her a fortune. Annie was always so generous with money; she was like a dream big sister in a film, revealing the thrills of London. It was also when I had my first McDonald's, at the one on Villiers Street which was still there until a couple of years ago. To me it was like eating in the future. I'd heard of McDonald's but never seen one (hard to imagine, but they didn't have them outside London back then). The thin French fries in a tiny cardboard box; the apple pie that wasn't even the shape or texture of a pie; and the milkshake . . . my God, the milkshake! It was truly like something that only astronauts would have drunk. We had Nesquik at home – milk and a spoonful of pink (artificial strawberry flavour) powder. This milkshake was thick and huge and delicious. It had to have a special straw with a wider circumference than normal straws, because it was thicker than any drink that had ever been made! I can't stress enough how alien and impressive a McDonald's meal was in 1977.

On Sunday I had to get the train back to boarding school.

Annie told me to wear my own clothes on the train: 'You don't need to wear your uniform all the way. Change after Sheffield, just before the train gets into Chesterfield, and the nuns won't know. You could go to the bar and get a drink.' That was a fundamental difference between us. I didn't mind wearing my school uniform and I didn't want to try to buy a drink at the bar or talk to boys.

Drawing attention to myself was the last thing I wanted to do. I knew Annie would've enjoyed it, though, so I did it to please her. I was aware that we were different, that she was racing to be an adult and I wasn't. Not just because it was scary, but also because I wasn't really interested in things that adults did. It didn't seem much fun. They never climbed trees or played running-around games. It just seemed to involve a lot of sitting and talking.

She was much more advanced as a teenager than I was; she was desperate to be out in the world and having adventures. Devouring books, smoking, wearing scarves and saying things that sounded dangerous. *Jesus doesn't exist. I'm a communist now. I'm never getting married.* That sort of thing. This will sound weird and hippy-dippy, but I wonder if her DNA knew? Is that why she was so precocious? Did her DNA know that she would have a short life? Some people think about God when someone dies. I thought about DNA.

There's a story my mum likes to tell about Annie reprimanding Grandma for giving her baby food when she was eighteen months old. She wasn't a baby, she had declared. 'I want steak and stuff,' she shouted as she pounded her little fists on the highchair. She wanted to be treated like an adult. At eighteen months.

When we were living on the Air Force base in Nottingham-shire we went on our first family holiday where it was acknowledged that Annie was now a teenager, an almost-adult. She was maybe seventeen. We went to stay in a cottage in North Wales, and Annie was allowed to bring a friend with her. She brought Tanya. Tanya wasn't like her other friends. Tanya was intimidatingly grown-up. She'd only been at the convent for a year so was more worldly than Annie's other friends. She smoked Rothmans in front of her parents and was studying secretarial skills. There was a big divide in all schools then: those who were going on to university and higher education and those who were going to further education. Secretarial classes – 'office practice', as it was called – was for those not going to university. It seems such a stupid choice: all those secretarial skills would've been useful for everyone. So Tanya seemed different. She had a perfect Purdey-from-*The Avengers* haircut and wore flawless make-up every day. How had a thirty-five-year-old woman been admitted to school? I wondered. My parents were doing their best, allowing Annie to have some freedom, but God, it must have been hard taking moody seventeen-year-olds on holiday.

I was sharing a room with Tanya and Annie. I lay awake listening to every word they said after their night out in the local town of Bethesda. They'd gone to a pub, and then some local boys had walked with them to the park and they'd sat on the swings. I liked swings. I must ask Annie where these swings are, I thought. Then Annie and Tanya started giggling and letting out little shrieks. Annie talked about a boy trying to get into her trousers. Tanya said something about a boy getting into her bra. What was going on? I pictured Annie's trousers; she'd been wearing her navy blue Oxford bags, very nice trousers. I'd have liked a pair like that. Did the boy not have trousers of his own? What did he want with Annie's trousers? Annie said again that he really wanted to get into her trousers. What on earth was in my sister's trousers? What did boys in Bethesda want from her trousers?

10

The Only New Romantics
in the Village

Adam Warnes (looking straight out of Spandau Ballet)
and me, 1980 – can't you tell?

I had been able to keep Annie's illness to myself. I hadn't discussed it with anyone outside Annie's group. Then, in July, my friend Adam had a stroke.

Again I got the news by email.

From: Adam Warnes

To: Jo Caulfield

Sent: 10 July 2015

Subject:

Hi, just to let you know I have just got out of hospital having had a stroke. It has left me without energy, little use in my left hand, trouble walking and slurred speech and to add to it I have 'dangerously' high blood pressure. So things not at their best at the moment. Will let you know more soon. Hope all good with you. AD xxxx

Typical Adam understatement.

Adam is my oldest friend. We had been friends since I was fourteen. We had been New Romantic weirdos together in a small village in Rutland. When I was about twenty-four I split up with my boyfriend and went to stay on Adam's couch for a few nights. The few nights turned into us sharing a flat for five years. At certain points in my life Adam and I had been almost inseparable. He's that friend we all need who just gets you and makes you feel good about yourself.

Annie knew him well. We'd all gone on holiday to Sardinia together; Annie and Adam both ended up chasing after the same waiter. When he didn't succumb to Annie's advances she declared, 'He's not gay, Adam. He's clearly got learning difficulties. I think he's a bit simple.' The waiter ended up coming to London to see Adam and then living there permanently. Two years later he was voted Soho's Gay Barman of the Year. So definitely not 'simple'.

As teenagers Adam and I went down to a house party of Annie's in North London. We were in our New Romantic finery — a proud lacy mess of puffy shirts, contoured cheekbones and tartan. We thought that all of London would be dressed like us, and it was somewhat surprising (mortifying) that we were the only ones. I overheard Annie defending us: 'They live in Rutland — it's very new there.'

That was the party where Annie learned that she didn't know how to make baked potatoes. I know! You would think the clue was in the name. She'd thought they'd be a great idea for cheap party food so she bought a sack of potatoes. These were then washed and parboiled, then put under a grill, then boiled again, then put in a bucket and stared at. Then we all started drinking. We went back to the bucket and fished some out, then arranged these semi-cooked, slimy potato bullets onto a plate and covered them in cheese. We then watched, horrified but fascinated, as people attempted to eat them.

Adam was shy but very handsome and very cool. He liked David Bowie, The Human League, Bauhaus and Boy George. He wore make-up and — cliché alert — he was also a huge fan of Barbra Streisand. Adam wasn't my boyfriend; I knew he couldn't be my boyfriend but I didn't quite know why. This was the late seventies — in Rutland. We didn't really know what being gay was.

I met Adam when I had to change school unexpectedly in fifth form. I had been at the convent in Matlock since I was eight. My dad had trouble finding a job after he left the Air Force and couldn't afford the fees, so I had to go to the local comprehensive. I'll never forget sitting in the car park at the convent as my dad went in to ask the Reverend Mother if they'd let me remain at school without paying the fees, just for the fifth form, so that I could take my O-levels. They said no. So much for Christian charity, the money-grabbing fuckers.

As weird as the convent was, when it came down to it I didn't want to leave. My friends were all there and I was about to go into my exam year. It was my brother James who told me that I wouldn't be going back after the summer holidays. I was glad that James had pre-warned me; I had a couple of days to get used to the idea. When my dad told me that I'd be going to a new school in a few days' time, the predominant thought in my head was that I mustn't cry. I mustn't make things worse for my parents by being upset. The tears came anyway; I couldn't stop them. I didn't make any noise, though. I just sat on my bed trying not to react as tears poured down my cheeks. Now, that seems horrifically unhealthy, and I feel for my younger self, but for some reason what was at the forefront of my mind was: don't get upset. I knew my dad didn't have a job and that life was now uncertain and different. I also knew that, if I got upset, my dad would feel bad, which would lead to shouting – and then everyone would feel bad. I just had to suck it up. But was there also a part of me that was absorbing this scene, the drama of it? Was the future writer/performer making notes? Possibly being a bit dramatic?

With hindsight I'm glad I left the convent then and went to a normal day school. The world opened up, and I think I might've been very weird if I'd stayed there till I was eighteen. Or *weirder* at least.

Adam was important in my life; he gave me confidence at that difficult time. I had suddenly lost all my anchors: Annie was at university in London, James was working in Scotland and I'd lost my friends from boarding school. Things were unsettled; things were going on that I didn't understand. My dad was drinking and was often in bed all day, and there were money worries. Adam thought I was funny, and we became friends, which meant that I made friends with his friends and wasn't just the freaky ex-convent girl who had suddenly showed up at the local comprehensive in the fifth form. Adam and I each had our own reasons for being just friends. The nuns had left me terrified of having a boyfriend; basically I believed that boyfriends made you pregnant and the shame of that would kill your parents.

We flounced about the village in berets and clothes we'd made from curtains. We smoked black Sobranie cigarettes and drank vodka and lime, but we were both ridiculously innocent and childish, really. Adam was older than me and could drive, and having a friend who drives is huge currency when you live in a village. He drove a carload of us to see The B-52's in London at the Hammersmith Palais. I didn't tell my parents. I knew I wouldn't be allowed to go so I hadn't asked permission. That was my logical thought process. Somehow I hadn't thought about the trouble that would be unleashed when we arrived back in Rutland at three o'clock in the morning.

'Where have you been?'

'Hammersmith Palais, London.'

'What?'

I was in huge trouble.

Adam opened my mind, in the same way that Annie did, to everything that wasn't the norm: John Waters, Divine, Andy Warhol. He held parties in the village hall (he was very good

Headless space girl. I had hoped to wear this homemade
ensemble to the Futurama music festival in Leeds, in 1979, but
I wasn't allowed to go. Joy Division, Public Image Ltd, OMD,
A Certain Ratio and Cabaret Voltaire are just some of the
bands I didn't get to see that weekend.

at doing parties). There were invitations and a dress code and
an entry fee of a pound. In the photo of me wearing a black
bin bag as a dress – at the time I was going for Siouxsie Sioux;
well, not even that really, I was copying cool girls who were
going for Siouxsie Sioux – I achieved 'girl looking awkward
in a black bin bag'. Another time, he had a toga party, and I
spent the whole night feeling extremely vulnerable because
I didn't wear any pants. For some reason I thought that was
what you did at toga parties. It had been a real dilemma before
the party. What if there was some sort of pants inspection and
then I would look really uncool for wearing pants.

Although nearly everyone was underage, you could buy cider and beer at the bar. I suppose it was run by village-hall volunteers who would rather their children got drunk in 'a safe place', but there were always older blokes from the pub lurking along the walls and by the bar. The whole thing would probably be a huge safeguarding issue nowadays.

★

I thought it was just a thing people said: that men don't go to the doctor. Adam hadn't been to a doctor in twenty-five years. You know how they always take your blood pressure? Turns out that's really important. Adam had crazily high blood pressure, had probably had it for years, as they think he had already had a stroke without knowing it. The stress of moving from London to Rutland was too much. When they got him to the hospital he said that they kept taking his blood pressure. It was so high that it set off an alarm. Adam decided that the system was flawed – an alarm going off is guaranteed to make your blood pressure go up. He was in a macabre comedy sketch of endless alarms and rocketing blood pressure.

I met my friend Gill for coffee. Gill knows Annie and Adam. Gill, Adam and I had all worked in a restaurant together in the late eighties. I told her about Annie and Adam. Finally, I told someone else. I had to tell someone. 'I can't lose them both,' I said. Tears came into Gill's eyes. I thought, 'I shouldn't have told her; it's too much to lay on someone,' but I also thought, 'I'm not actually going to lose either of them, so there's nothing to cry about.' It was all getting too dramatic. It wasn't like anyone was actually going to die.

11

Ben Sherman Shirts and Shoplifting

RAF Coltishall, Norfolk, 1972. Annie is thirteen. James (before his growth spurt) is eleven, in his favourite 'Jason King' safari suit.

Annie was getting better. Her hair had grown back and grown back beautifully. Like me Annie had been dyeing her hair for so long that neither of us had any idea what our natural colour was. She was afraid it would grow back grey – 'like that awful *Daily Mail* woman' (I think she meant Melanie Phillips, no offence, Melanie) – but it grew back a wonderful chestnut brown, rich and glossy. I was interested to see what our hair colour was. The steroids had made her gain weight and pushed out any wrinkles. She was looking better than she had in years. We joked about what a good beauty treatment a course of chemo and steroids could be.

She was able to go in for a day at Goldsmiths' College, where she was a 'royal literary thingy', as she called it. She went there once a month to have sessions with her clients/students, a job she liked because it was paid and it wasn't teaching creative writing. It was helping people who weren't writers – scientists, sociologists and historians – to write essays, which she found interesting.

She never wanted to teach creative writing, and it's probably good that she never did. Her view was that they should just tell all the students to fuck off and write. It's not the worst advice for would-be writers, but it's maybe not the best way of putting it.

Goldsmiths didn't know she had cancer. I think she told them something else . . . an illness, but not cancer. She was hoping to be able to do this one day of work and then have the summer to get well. She thought there was no need to bother people with her cancer.

Dr Tom said she was strong enough to go away for a few days' holiday. Annie and Martin decided to go to Norfolk, to Hunstanton on the coast. We had lived in Norfolk twice when we were kids (on different Air Force bases), in what Martin thought of as our idyllic *Swallows and Amazons* middle-class childhood. Martin's childhood had been spent in a council flat in Battersea, and he would take the piss out of Annie when she complained about her childhood: 'Your parents rented a rowing boat on the Norfolk Broads? What bastards!'

It was in Norfolk that she'd started shoplifting – when she was a teenager, not as a side effect from chemo as an adult. She was in her 'suedehead' phase, inspired by the book of the same name published in 1971 by Richard Allen, so this would have been about 1972, when Annie was thirteen or fourteen. Her world was a Catholic boarding school in Derbyshire and an Air Force base in East Anglia – how she discovered a series of books about 'bovver boys' I have no idea. And that is what they were called – 'bovver boys'. It sounds like something from an old public information film: 'Watch out for bovver boys, often found congregating in town centres.' The author was actually a man called Jim Moffat, a fifty-year-old British-Canadian pulp-fiction author who, under different pen names, wrote hundreds of books in various genres from his cottage in Sidmouth, Devon.

She'd got a short-sleeved Ben Sherman shirt for her birthday and a knitted tank top. I remember all the details about what she read and what she wore very clearly: they were just some of the hundreds of things that I would make mental notes of, the things Annie likes that I don't know about but should probably like, too.

We went into the NAAFI (the shop on an RAF camp). It was the only place for miles on an Air Force base where a precocious teenager like Annie might find . . . something. Not even something to do, but something that maybe wasn't this small, familiar beige world. When we came out to the car park she had something in her hand. We hadn't bought anything.

She rolled it around in her hand cockily, waiting to be asked how she had something in her hand when we hadn't bought anything.

'I stole it,' she snarled. She held up a small roll of blue surgical tape.

There wasn't anything cool like make-up or records to steal in the NAAFI, but that hadn't spoiled her plans; she improvised on her would-be delinquent bovver girl fantasy. As always, she was writing a life for herself, a different, more exciting life.

Obviously, bovver boys were few and far between in the officers' married quarters, but she did have access to another type of rebel – fairground boys. A couple of times a year we were taken to the funfair at Great Yarmouth, a proper big one with a rollercoaster and poor people. My parents thought Annie was old enough to look after me and James, so while they went to the pub, we ran along behind Annie doing whatever we were told. It was around the time that the David Essex film *That'll Be the Day* came out. James and I were forced to go round and round on the Waltzers in the hope that fairground boys would jump on the back. Annie lit up with excitement. I didn't, I was terrified. 'Do you wanna go faster?' the fairground boy shouted. 'No, thank you,' I said, very politely and primly.

Annie never spoke to the fairground boys, though. She wasn't confident in that way, but in her imagination she was – the Annie that she wanted to be wouldn't have been shy and awkward, so she would pretend that she was a different Annie.

'See the one with the earring? He's called Glen. He spoke to me, gave me a sign.' He hadn't, and I knew he hadn't, but that wasn't important. Glen was her favourite name for boys at that time. There were lots of Glens. This is all mixed up with my memory of us watching the film *Sky West and Crooked*, with Hayley Mills, and Ian McShane as the handsome gypsy boy (I still think it's a lovely film). Annie was always interested in anything that was 'other' – anything that might be part of the bigger life that she was going to lead when she was old enough.

Dr Tom said she was going to be able to travel again, to make it to Cambodia, if she took it easy and built up her strength. For the rest of the autumn she really worked on eating and sleeping and getting strong again. We met for tea a few times and she was really happy and excited about her trip. We had always swapped books, so I often took along some books.

I had found a Norman Lewis novel in a second-hand shop. He is one of scores of writers that Annie introduced me to, and she'd bought me *Naples '44* for my birthday one year. Lewis had been stationed in Italy at the end of the Second World War, when Naples was rubble and people were starving. The book is interesting historically, but also full of stories of intrigue and vendettas. A lot of his work was out of print, so if I found a new Norman Lewis book, it was a little thing that could perk her up.

Anne of Green Gables was the first book that I really remember enjoying, and Annie had recommended it. I'd been reading *Pollyanna*, which adults kept telling me was a great book but which I thought was boring (I was also quite jealous of Pollyanna, who seemed to have a great life and naturally blonde hair). 'What do they know?' Annie had said in her cool twelve-year-old way. Who says that? Don't adults know everything?

The other book that was very confusing to me as a child was Enid Blyton's *The Naughtiest Girl in the School*. I would've been about eight when I excitedly got it out of the library. On the cover was a drawing of a girl of about fourteen in a school uniform holding a handwritten sign that said 'The Naughtiest Girl in the School'. She looked very cool. Annie had filled my head with stories about all the fun things she got up to at the convent; therefore the naughtiest girl in the school was, in my mind, bound to be the coolest and most popular girl in school. So what was this shit I was reading? According to Enid Blyton, the naughtiest girl in the school wasn't popular, wasn't considered cool and didn't have any friends. Oh yeah? Enid, you could not have got it more wrong. I didn't even finish the book. It turned out the sign on the cover saying 'The Naughtiest Girl in the School' was a punishment, not an accolade.

Dr Tom had said he would get her well enough to go to Cambodia and finish her book, and he had done it. I was worried about her going there alone when she wasn't fully fit, but she said she was better on her own, she had a writing routine when she was travelling, and having another person around would just get in her way. She then added: 'It's not like I have an illness or anything. I just have cancer.'

Okay . . .

'Don't worry, dear,' she said.

We had called each other 'dear' ever since we'd had a brief infatuation with the TV show *Mapp & Lucia* (the 1985 version with Geraldine McEwan, Prunella Scales and Nigel Hawthorne). Saying vicious things in a quaint seaside town, who wouldn't want to be part of that? We imagined being those ladies when we were old, how we could quite happily live like that, maybe next door to each other – two delightfully mad old bats.

Every now and again we would both get obsessed with the same TV show. The first one was *Brideshead Revisited* – it was

1981 and I had just moved to London. I was working as a breakfast waitress at the Tara Thistle Hotel; it's still there, a big place behind Kensington High Street. The job came with staff accommodation in a hostel. I thought I was set for life: a job and somewhere to live. I had a room in a big house in Notting Hill Gate, sharing with a girl from Dublin, Mary. Mary was studying hotel management and was very sophisticated. She was always talking about going to nightclubs and hanging out with rich men – men who'd buy you champagne. I had nothing to add to the conversation: I was a rockabilly and was going out with a boy who worked in the hotel laundry who was also a rockabilly. And I drank Harp lager. Mary was a different species to me: she was sexy and confident, and she said she liked rich Arabs best as they didn't expect to have sex with you, you could just sleep together. To this day I've no idea what that really means.

'You know that way, Jo? When you don't have to perform.'

'Oh yes,' I said. Completely clueless.

She had long, straight chesnut brown hair. I was mesmerised by her hair; we'd wake up in our single beds and her hair would just swing round in a glossy, perfect sheet, ready for the day.

We were both eighteen, but she wore what seemed like adults' clothing, blouses and slacks. High-heeled court shoes under the slacks and high-necked blouses with a pearl necklace at the collar like Princess Diana. Power dressing for the life she wanted, I suppose, and she already knew exactly what she wanted from life. A big house, expensive clothes and a Mercedes car. I had no idea what I wanted. I didn't even know that it was something you should think about at eighteen. As different as we were, we got on really well. She was funny and daring, and she'd offer to take me with her to the 'rich men nightclubs': 'Obviously you'd need to wear some of my clothes, you'll be grand.' It wasn't for me; I didn't understand the dynamic. Why this fun young girl wanted to hang out with conservative thirty-year-old men in suits. I hope she got the big house and the Mercedes. I'm sure she did.

Annie was renting a room in one of the big four-storey houses down the hill in Holland Park. The owners were an older couple who had made money in South America, and it was all very post-colonial. The man was old and posh, with that weathered look of a man who'd spent his life in 'the Tropics'; his wife was from Chile and was 'a character'. The husband would say she was 'a character', and then she would dance about or sing and show what a crazy character she was. The house seemed to be decorated mostly in red and orange, with huge pieces of teak furniture and swords dangling precariously from the walls. At first they adored having Annie and treated her like a daughter, but we came to think it was just a whim, having a lodger. Maybe they needed someone to show off to, a captive audience for the wife to be a character in front of, because quite soon it got a bit dark. They became petty and controlling, and Annie ended up getting thrown out for spilling Alpen on the carpet.

Before that happened I used to go down the hill from the hostel every Sunday night. We'd have a bottle of wine, watch *Brideshead Revisited* and talk about it afterwards. I didn't understand a lot of what Annie said about it and I don't remember why we liked it so much. It was a period drama, but it seemed modern and groundbreaking, with new and exciting actors. Jeremy Irons was new and exciting then. It was a comforting thing to do when you're eighteen and have just moved to London. How cosy and fun to watch glamorous people on telly with your big sister when you're living in a hostel and working as a breakfast waitress. *Twin Peaks*, *Prisoner Cell Block H*, *Buffy the Vampire Slayer*, *Southland*, *Come Dine with Me*, *The Wire*, *Oz*, *Peaky Blinders*, *Girls* and *Vikings* were other shows I remember us raving about to each other. And *Mapp & Lucia*, of course.

Annie emailed a couple of times from Cambodia. Very short emails, just a line, usually about the heat and how she was exhausted but happy. I was glad to get them, glad to know she was okay.

12

Waistcoats and Bow Ties

Dad dressed up for Christmas dinner. Annie had
bought him his namesake William bear.

It was 4 December, and I was doing a gig in Worcester. My plan
was to visit Mum and Dad the next day. When I got back to the
hotel there were four missed calls from my brother. I phoned his
mobile. Daddy had had a heart attack and died almost instantly.
His heart just gave out. I was shocked because I thought he
would go on being vaguely ill for years. I also felt guilty because
I thought, 'Oh fuck, looks like you really were ill.'

He was eighty-two, and, like they say, that's not a bad age.
I think my dad had had enough; it was upsetting to think that

he thought that about life. I felt sad for my mum and I felt sad for myself. That relationship was done now; it couldn't ever be worked out. I grieved for the dad I would've liked to have had as well as for the good times I'd had with the dad I'd had. He wasn't the easiest person, but I loved him. He was my dad.

I'd bought his Christmas present two days earlier, spent ages picking out a turquoise moleskin waistcoat – he loved bright clothes with a hint of the flamboyant. I'd kept the receipt in case it was the wrong size. It's funny the inappropriate thoughts you have at these times. I thought I couldn't really take it back and say, 'Actually, he died, so he doesn't need it any more – can I have a refund?' Could I? My mum said it was perfect for the funeral so she gave it to the undertaker along with his favourite striped shirt and bow tie. I did think, 'So you're just going to burn this perfectly good waistcoat?' Somehow it seemed unfair on the waistcoat. But my dad had liked clothes, often spending far too much money (when we didn't have much money) on tailor-made suits, so it was fitting that my mum took time to put together a nice final outfit for him.

I was grateful for Mum's old friends coming to visit her. She'd been with my dad for sixty years. They were friends at university in Belfast before they became a couple, and he was the love of her life. He was handsome and glamorous with his English accent in Belfast, although the fact that my dad had an English accent despite having grown up in West Belfast (and not in the leafy suburbs of Belfast but just off the Crumlin Road) should have rung alarm bells. He always said it was because his mother was from the Clonmel and she didn't want him having a Belfast accent.

The nice side of my dad was that he was eccentric and

different. Why not adopt an English accent if you're pretending to be David Niven or Dirk Bogarde? The not-so-nice side of my dad meant that he thought his assumed accent made him superior, so he was always putting on airs and could be infuriatingly pretentious. Charming and interesting but with a quick temper that could change the mood of the house in an instant.

My mum just let it wash over her, but I don't want you to think she was downtrodden. She wasn't. No, to her it was just what you had to put up with because that was part of who he was, and she loved who he was. And she thought everyone else should, too. My mum loved him unconditionally. She would say with a laugh, 'You've got to love him or murder him – you can't change him.' Is that really the two choices you want in life, though?

There was always a lot of tension between Annie and my dad. One Christmas, when she was about nineteen, she arrived home drunk for Midnight Mass. She had started drinking on the train from London and came clanking into the church, giggling and singing. Drowning out the poor choirboy's solo by happily yelling along to 'Once In Royal David's City'; she then looked around with mock innocence, nudged me and gave a big stage wink. She was thoroughly enjoying herself. It all came to a head later at home. I can't remember what was said but my dad ended up blasting her with the soda syphon – what a very seventies dysfunctional family image.

But I understand what my mum loved about him. On a visit home once, she was at her bridge club so Dad and I had the evening on our own together. He was funny and relaxed, and I really enjoyed his company. When he had your undivided attention he was a different person. He was an only child. His father had died when he was twelve, and then he was raised by his mum and her sister, my great-aunt Josie. Who knew what that was like. Maybe he had just never learned to share.

We planned the funeral. The undertaker had an easy, down-to-earth manner, and it made us laugh when my mum said, 'Well, we'll definitely use him again.' She laughed when I pointed out that that would most likely be for her funeral.

Annie was back from Cambodia, and she and Martin were coming up from London on the train for the funeral. To Annie this was good timing, because Mum would see her looking well and would never need to know about the cancer.

When I went into the front room at my mum's and asked James if he knew what time Annie was coming, he said, 'Annie's not coming. She's had a seizure.'

'What?'

That morning, the morning of Dad's funeral, she had gone into convulsions and was taken to hospital. I couldn't react because I couldn't let Mum know what had happened; it all became sort of farcical. Molly was now going to attend the funeral as Annie's representative (whatever that meant), and the plan was to tell Mum that Annie had some sort of weird Cambodian dysentery, bad enough that you had to go to hospital. It was the only plan we could come up with. Molly was brilliant at the funeral. She got on with all the relatives who'd come over from Northern Ireland and said lovely things about my dad. It was a success. Only James, Molly and I knew why Annie wasn't there. What did seizures mean? I was burying my father but thinking about my sister.

Despite all of this going on, James helped conduct the service and delivered an amazing eulogy – funny and honest, the best kind. I wanted to read a poem, but the parish priest said I had to read a psalm or something from the Gospels. James, as a priest himself, said it's kind of the parish priest's decision, that it's sort of a 'his ball, his rules' kind of deal. So I didn't. The readings for funerals are usually terrible. It's all 'we're fuck-ups', 'we're sinners', ' Lord have mercy on us all for being such terrible people' and 'we come into the world alone and we go out alone'. Dear Catholic Church, you need to update your approach to celebrating the dead.

We stumbled through Christmas. My husband and I went down and stayed with Mum at James's house. She wasn't really processing anything, so she didn't seem to question Annie having 'dysentery' for such an insane amount of time.

Annie's 'dysentery' was a brain tumour. I know now that's what happens with lung cancer; cancer cells enter the blood-stream or the lymph nodes and travel to the brain. But Little Miss Ignorant didn't know that then; Annie said they could operate and it would all be fine, and I believed her.

I went to visit her on 6 January, the day after the operation. She was sitting up in bed with a big comedy bandage round her head and demanding her laptop. She wanted to work on her Cambodia book. She was thrilled that her brain was still working, amazed that, post-neurosurgery, she was still able to write. She said she was having some freaky brain activity, hallu-cinating, most of which was probably due to her meds. All this strange behaviour fascinated her.

'I thought one of the paramedics was Jesus,' she said. 'But I knew it was a test and I had to work out which one was really Jesus. One of them had a beard; apparently I kept telling him that I knew it wasn't him – it would be too obvious if Jesus had a beard. They said I was tapping my nose at him knowingly saying, "You're not Jesus, you're not fooling me."'

Annie loved her brain. No, that's too arrogant; she *cherished* it, like an acrobat might cherish their body, because of all the things it could do. Writers live in their brains more than most people; they spend time there, waiting for things to form, looking for the right words. I listened to a programme on Radio 4 about the writer Muriel Spark; a friend of hers said that Muriel believed in an afterlife but had said she only wanted a short visit to heaven, a weekend stay, as she wanted to come back and write about it. I could totally relate to that idea. Annie was always talking about what she would write when she got better, always writing in her head. Like Muriel Spark wanting to write about heaven, she would have written about her illness if she had come out the other side. Everything was material to Annie.

She believed that your brain was you, it was your essence or soul, so it was vitally important to her that her brain, despite surgery, was still *her*, and that no matter what cancer did to her, she was still 'herself'.

Here's a piece about writing that Annie wrote for *Standard Issue* magazine.

Busy Doing Nothing

There's an old *Oxford Dictionary of Quotations* chestnut about writers from American journalist Burton Rascoe: 'What no wife of a writer can ever understand is that a writer is working when he's staring out of the window.'

I know.'He'? And I live with a male writer who would never *dare* refer to me in any 'little woman wouldn't understand' fashion. But I've always hoped the window-staring thing was true. This week I might have proved it.

Because I had so much to do, I sat at the computer then stared out of the window. Not just any window: French windows. Someone could run through them at any moment and begin a bedroom farce. Do people still say French windows? I hear talk of patio doors but did the French window go off with Ben Travers into the glazing hereafter? Of course, now I also have to know why they're French.

Were people less easily distracted before they could go online? Not necessarily. The moment I discover all I can about French windows, I look out through mine again and see a horrible thing. Then I know the day is doomed.

Oh, and by the way, the term French window seems to be interchangeable with French door but applies to the small-paned, wood-framed openings in an exterior wall. Whereas, a patio door is a sheet of glass, usually sliding onto the outside area . . .

So, outside my small-paned French windows I have a container garden. The plants form a barrier, defending what I have decided is my section of the terrace behind our flats. No one else has bothered to fence themselves in like this; perhaps it's just that I have more time on my hands . . . No, I don't. I have a sitcom pilot to write.

But, but . . . there, making its way across the terrace, it's a small, fat, rat.

I give up on work and find the caretaker.

Rats, he says, are above his pay grade. Specialists have to be called. Meanwhile, not to worry: 'Remember, they're more scared of you than you are of them.'

I thank him for this, although it isn't true. Otherwise, wouldn't I see the rat on the other side of the French windows flapping at a rat caretaker?

The caretaker promises rat-catchers; I go back to work on the script. It seems disappointingly lifeless. All too easy to spurn writing and watch the two men in overalls laying black plastic boxes along the back wall.

'Traps,' the men tell me.

When the men are gone, I go out to inspect. One hole in the black plastic box. Is the rat beheaded in there, or just trapped until it starves to death, suffocates, has a stress-induced heart attack? What if I have to sit and watch the flailing tail of a dying rodent while trying to do something with a dying sitcom?

The next morning, the caretaker tells me, 'You know what the rat-catchers were saying is really the only thing that works? Get a cat.'

My neighbours think I'm odd enough; I'm not giving them 'with a cat' to add to the way they talk about me.

I try to work. I wonder what they're called these days instead of rat-catchers? *Pest Control* it said on the van. I don't like the incomplete implications of 'control'. Eradication, annihilation, or pest extinction would be more reassuring.

I move sitcom characters through mud for a while, then I drift. The old profession of rat-catcher reminds me of a friend who lives in a historic Derbyshire village; what was it she told me about an eccentric job up there that has something to do with rats? I have to email her. Yes, there's a man called a *lengthsman*. He goes through the village tidying the verges and reporting potholes. The village has had one since medieval times when the area was being decimated by bubonic plague. The lengthsman had to catch and burn any rats found in the thoroughfares. No, she doesn't know if the lengthsman is a job unique to her village ... I Google *lengthsman*. Well, well: lengthsmen are returning to rural areas. They clear verges, gutters and maintain village greens; the priority alert for plague rats seems to have died down.

A lengthsman. Something of the bedroom farce echoes in this job title. Or perhaps more *Carry On* film. There's a cackle of Sid James' laughter every time I type the word.

With great excitement I realise I may be typing it frequently.

The lead character in my sitcom knew everyone and everything because she worked part-time in the village shop. This is why there was a stuck-mud feel to the drama. If my character is the newly appointed lengthswoman, thus moving around the village, doing various tasks while she gets to know everyone, there's action, surprise, unwieldy comedy implements ...

I know I'll take advantage of all this, excusing myself from the desk within five minutes of trying to write the next difficult script. 'Remember the lengthsmen!' I'll tell myself, as I skive and slither, free as a rat in a sewer.

There may be an art to finding the usefulness in window staring, a balance that has to be calculated every day. Tomorrow there may be no creative journey to follow in the tail of a rat. How will I know until I've followed? How will I know when I'll just be jet-blasted into an oblivion of wasted time? Even in being distracted from work, there's work. The best I can hope for is control of the pest. Something rat-catchers clearly resigned themselves to a long time ago.

13

Saying Fuck on Radio 4

Annie looking devilish, 1990.

Annie was totally energised with the relief of having come through the surgery and told me excitedly that she had planned her funeral. It made me feel unsteady on my feet when she said that. I inwardly tensed, my heart contracted and I kept looking at her expression, trying to read her mood, not from what she was saying but from how she looked. She was laughing and happy, so I laughed, too. She said she'd enjoyed doing it, that it was like a writing exercise, and everything would be sorted for Martin; the funeral arrangements would keep him busy.

No one was talking about the possibility of her dying, but this shows that the thought was in her head. Being Annie, she couldn't leave the ending to chance, have other people write the end. No, she would finish her own narrative. She also said that Martin should meet somebody else because 'he's a very good boyfriend'.

She wasn't really a practical person in many ways, but I think she did this at exactly the right time: plan your funeral and talk to your loved ones when it is in the abstract, when you still have hope.

It was important to Annie to keep making plans, to keep thinking through writing projects. She had her brilliant brain and it was still in full working order. She took huge comfort from her doctor saying to her: 'You're still the same woman I met sixteen months ago; you're still exactly "yourself".' She repeated this a lot; it must have meant a great deal.

On 10 January 2016, a few days after Annie's surgery, David Bowie died. To most people who had grown up between the sixties and the eighties, Bowie dying was a big deal – not in a crazy-fan-crying way but because he was a foundation stone in our lives. Of course for me it wasn't just about him, it was about him and the association with Annie. Bowie was an influence on many musicians and artists, but he was also a huge inspiration to little girls who were attracted to people who were different and interesting.

I can see us both in Chelsea Girl, in the Broadmarsh Shopping Centre in Nottingham. Culottes were a thing, culottes worn with knee-length boots. Annie had a pair in bottle green corduroy, and I'd been amazed that Mum had bought her knee-length leather boots. We were busy looking longingly at denim culottes when 'Space Oddity' came on (it would have been the 1975 reissue). Annie told me that this was David Bowie, and I obediently made a mental note to remember this Bowie bloke, with his croaky, reedy voice sing-ing about a junkie. There was a dark side to life, and she taught me that that's where the interesting people are and where the interesting things happen. Or so we thought then.

Shortly after Bowie's death, a magazine asked contributors to write about their two favourite Bowie songs. These are Annie's, and she wrote this just days after having brain surgery.

'Rock 'N' Roll Suicide' and 'Ashes To Ashes'

In my shallow, punky youth I was in a bar with some friends. Someone slightly older came in and said that John Lennon had been shot. I pouted and shrugged and said, 'Means nothing to me. If David Bowie died, then I'd care.'

My friends agreed. The older person swore at us and left us to our pints of Snakebite.

I won't waste time here telling you why The Beatles leave me cold. I want to celebrate the liberating individuality of Bowie. He made sexual fluidity, and a self-defining explor-ation of your right to be anything, into a thing that could happen. Way back when everything was teak veneer and fawn wallpaper.

Bowie came the closest any human being has ever been to making mime cool. (He failed. It *is* impossible, but he did nearly manage it.)

If I had to choose a song? In my self-dramatising but really pretty depressed early teens I would sit in my bedroom chain-smoking and playing the single 'Rock 'N' Roll Suicide', over and over again.

I was not alone.

And more importantly this piece of private theatre kept me busy, let out how I felt and very likely stopped me from doing something truly stupid.

Now I've grown up to be cynical but very perky, so I'd choose the cynical yet perky 'Ashes To Ashes'.

The lyrics are deftly about how being a junkie and giving up trying is a bad idea. Or you'll never do bad things. But you'll never do good things. And life is there to be engaged with, by the likes of us.

To get things done, you better not mess with Major Tom.

Don't let the fuckwits of the world send you into shut-down and retreat. Get things done. Like David did.

I can see her sitting in our Air Force house in the middle of nowhere, playing 'Rock 'n' Roll Suicide' and mouthing lyrics about time taking a cigarette and putting it in your mouth. She smoked, but she didn't smoke in her bedroom. My parents wouldn't have allowed that. They both smoked then, so she would lean out the window in the upstairs toilet, somehow thinking my parents would think it was their smoke. Of course now I see how ridiculous that was because my parents didn't smoke in the toilet in their own house. She would make me go for 'smoking walks' with her; sometimes she didn't have any cigarettes and it was just about getting away. Taking me swimming was a way of escaping. This involved walking three miles across a muddy field to the Bingham baths. I would swim and she would sit in the café, hoping life would happen. And if nothing happened, she would invent a story, a fantasy of what had happened in the café.

You couldn't be sure you'd have friends to play with in the school holidays. Our friends from boarding school went back to wherever their parents lived, scattered all over the world. There were some kids my age on this base but no one of Annie's age. We came back from school to a new house in a new place with new people.

A boy called Malcolm used to go to the café in the leisure centre. He had a denim bomber jacket and flared turquoise satin trousers, and was as close as Bingham swimming baths got to a resident Marc Bolan. We learned a lesson from Malcolm: satin trousers do not necessarily an interesting person make. When I asked him his name I swear he spelled it out like you would in infant school, 'Malc. M-A-L-C.'

Sometimes, someone's trousers are the best thing about them.

Get things done. That could have been Annie's motto. She liked to get up at six in the morning and write. It was the best time, she said, because there were no emails or distraction. Just coffee and your brain. She always worked hard, she had such a strong work ethic, and she was hugely irritated by people who said that they 'wanted to be writers' or that they 'thought they might have a book in them'. It's something people feel entitled to say to writers, not realising how insulting it actually is. If you met an architect, you wouldn't say, 'I think I've got a multi-use development in me. Yeah, I might design one – it's just finding the time.' Nor would you say to a teacher, 'I always thought I'd be a great teacher. I've got a way with kids, y'know. Maybe I'll give it a go one day.'

As well as her Cambodia book, Annie had a commission to adapt Erica Jong's *Fear of Flying* for Radio 4's *Woman's Hour*.

There was a lot of press around it because they were going to say 'fuck' on Radio 4 at eleven in the morning. Amazingly, she got the script finished in a few days after her operation. She was even more amazed when the producer praised her work. Annie said, 'It could possibly be the ravings of a mad woman. I've got a hole in my head.'

Then, in that same January, Martin's mother, Mary, died. She had been ill for some time: coming and going, sometimes conscious, sometimes not. Martin had been looking after both Annie and his mum. It must have been very hard, as he didn't have the time or emotional space to grieve for his mum. Annie loved Mary and had a great relationship with her. They had taken her to Spain with them, to their cave house in Northern Andalucía, and Annie had loved how grateful Mary was, how easily pleased. Sitting in the sun with her large-print Catherine Cookson, Mary would say to Annie that she felt like a queen.

The cave house needs some explanation. It sounded to me like a hole in a mountain that they bought for, thankfully, not very much money.

Here's how Annie described it . . .

Unusual Places to Live

'You bought a what?'

   'A cave house.'

   'A what?'

   'Ugh, all dark and clammy?''

   'Living in a cave? Like Flintstones? Like Hobbits? Like bears?'

I'd seen pictures but I'd not really understood cave houses either, until I owned one.

My partner had seen them on a travel show and became obsessed. He found some rental caves and dragged me away by the hair.

Well, not really, but I had a bad feeling I'd be climbing a rope ladder up a cliff face to get to my bed, which was just as annoying.

At first glance the row of caves appeared to be simple white cottages built against the hillside. From the front they looked normal. From the side they were strangely narrow and would only work as cottages for very, very thin people, with furniture that folded flat while in use. But the cave was behind the cottage front, stretching back and back into the hillside, for people to be as rounded out in as they needed to be.

The rental cave, cute and chintzy inside, was the sort of place where any Beatrix Potter creature would have felt at home. There was hand carved furniture, a log fire, bright ceramic jugs and bowls; gingham curtains . . .

I thought we'd be creeping about with lanterns, even in the middle of the afternoon, but there was natural light in the bathroom, kitchen and dining area at the front of the cave. Going back into the hill, through the small living room to the bedroom, the white, rough plastered walls expanded the light coming from strong bulbs hidden behind latticed terracotta tiles to make subtly bright rooms ...

It was the darkness and silence of the cave night that kept me awake. A city girl, I couldn't find this level of darkness in my memory. Anything could have been going on inches in front of our faces and we wouldn't know about it. Till it grabbed us.

Maybe I could get used to the nights but I worried about the daytime psychology of cave life ... wouldn't cave dwelling make the modern person who knew the word for 'depression' sink way down?

Not in Andalucía, where the sunlight felt powerful enough to crack rock. What people needed for at least half the year was to hide from the mind-frying daylight. Besides, there were caves with skylights; caves that went up several well-windowed storeys; caves that curved round a mountain with windows all along ...

Many of the caves for sale were as cutely refurbished as our rental cave. Or they were long, low rock holes. Like the one we bought. For next to nothing, mind you. And it has its own field by a stream in the valley below.

The main charm of our used hole in the ground is the view. Northern Andalucía has a stark, Middle-Eastern landscape with flashes of blue and green mountain lakes. Or swathes of olive trees beside whitewashed villages ...

We watched the sun go down over the valley. We heard the bells tinkling on a flock of goats being driven home. Like all the hills of the region, the hills opposite had chimneys dotted about. We seemed to be the last house in the village but the underground population spread for miles.

Down on the roadside below us, a group of our neighbours,

old Spanish ladies in pinnies, accompanied by small yapping dogs, arrived pulling kitchen chairs, gathering to natter until the sun went down. They must have seen this so often but they paused for a while to watch the last blaze of the sunset. It was never the same two nights in a row. The old ladies and their dogs retreated to their caves for dinner and we sat out waiting for the clearest view of stars I've had in my life.

14

'Interesting Girls'

Annie and I at Bar Sol in Soho. I don't know what my
hair is meant to be doing. It was the late 1980s,
and I was morphing out of rockabilly.

Looking back through our emails, there were then some very
busy months. Some positive times. Annie went up to see Mum
in April of 2016. The agreement was that she was told about
this cancer but not about the lung cancer. Annie said there was
no reason to tell her about the lungs, 'they were better', and it
would only hurt Mum to know that we had kept it from her. So
we all just talked about the brain tumour, as if Annie having cancer was a new thing. When she went to Mum's she didn't have
a stick and looked well, but something had gone wrong with
her balance and she usually needed one. Without a stick, she

said, she just lurched off to the right until she toppled over into the nearest wall or group of strangers. It was one of those NHS walking sticks with the three-pronged base at the end. 'Annie 3 Prong' she called herself, like it was her First Nation name.

It must have taken superhuman effort to appear well for Mum. She was hugely relieved to have told her and to be able to have a relationship with her again instead of constantly avoiding her or having to invent lies about what she was up to.

She was swinging between days of strength and days of being wiped out. Now taking huge amounts of drugs to stop infection after the surgery as well as anti-seizure medication, she summed it up in an email: 'I am very emotional – very shouty, weepy, huggy, laughy, crazy and then sleepy.'

A physio was visiting every day to help her right side, to retrain her brain to do some simple things. She couldn't tie the laces on her trainers. My mum told her that as a child she'd had great difficulty learning to tie her laces. 'You were so smart, but I would watch your little face struggling to get dressed; the shoelaces never tied and your cardigan was always buttoned up wrong.' Annie found that comforting. It wasn't just the brain tumours; her brain had never liked doing these things.

I was finishing off my tour and had settled into my new house in Leith. We emailed frequently, and I was constantly trying to think of things she would enjoy. I had become a criminal, which I knew she would appreciate. Careering between Annie, sorting my dad's 'estate' (a messy, never-ending pile of bank statements and insurance policies in no sort of logical order), moving house, getting a kitchen and bathroom installed and touring the country, I'd forgotten to renew my car insurance. I'd been stopped on the motorway by a very officious and, frankly, threatening policeman. I was on my way to a gig in Manchester and avoided him impounding my car by renewing it there and then. It was a genuine mistake: with all that was going on in my life it had slipped my mind. But what I didn't realise was that the six points on my licence were 'special points'. Several months later, at the Enterprise rent-a-car desk at Birmingham airport, the man told me I was flagged. I had 'behavioural points', so was deemed a person who would behave badly in a hire car. Until those points were removed in six years' time, I would be unable to rent a car. Annie laughed at the vision of me behaving badly in a hire car. What even is behaving badly in a hire car? Moving the seats back and forth too much? Or necking vodka while chucking fast food wrappings around? Stopping in the emergency lane of the M1 to give blowjobs?

Our friend Adam was improving and hadn't been as badly damaged by the stroke as we'd first thought. I went to see him when I was down at Mum's. He was still staying in Rutland with his mother, Biddy, in the childhood home where I'd spent so much time as a teenager. A tale of recovery might be cheering for Annie, I thought. Biddy is a lot of fun, and I told Annie how she was a big fan of hers and listened to the World Service at night and often heard her radio plays. Biddy had kept saying what 'interesting girls' we were. She said it so often that Adam started laughing and said that she was making us sound odd rather than interesting. Biddy replied, 'Well, they are odd, and I like that. That's what makes them very interesting to me, interesting girls.' Annie liked being called 'an interesting girl' and I then got an ear worm for days of The Slits' song 'Typical Girls' but as 'Interesting Girls' . . . and now I've got it again.

Annie emailed that her old friend Dan had come over from America to visit his mother and they had met up. Dan had acted in, and then directed, some of Annie's plays and they'd remained friends even after he moved to LA. Dan had just left drama school when they first met, and they'd championed each other's work in the early days. They'd talked for six hours, but she didn't tell him anything about her illness, having decided 'there was no point boring him as it's in the past now anyway'. She was clearly thrilled to have seen him. We are so bombarded with messaging about how we should talk about everything at the moment, but sometimes it's just the talking that helps, not the talking about 'the thing'. She was right not to tell him.

Sometime in May or June of 2016, she went into Charing Cross Hospital, but my memory of this particular time was happy and hopeful. She was in a bright sunny room and was excited by the view. 'Look out the window, Joey. That's all of London out there.' It was an amazing view, and she told me about the staff and the handsome Spanish nurse who was making her feel much better. We went for a walk round the ward. She had her stick and needed to hold onto me but she was chattering and laughing as she banged into walls and stumbled about. Halfway through our wander, she realised her gown was open and that she'd been flashing everyone her tits. She cackled with delight.

Her bed was strewn with notebooks. She was working on an idea for a play about Bob Marley, and we talked about West London and going to the Notting Hill Carnival in the eighties. We reminisced about when she had worked in a warehouse under the Westway flyover, part of the building where Acklam

Hall is. If you're not of a certain age and weren't around London in the eighties, this won't have any resonance, but I'd like to describe it. That area around the bottom of Portobello and Ladbroke Grove was, to us, where cool things happened: where we mixed with people playing ska and reggae, where there were protests about everything, where we went to see bands and hung out in independent record shops and where we hoped to see The Clash walking around. We had definitely seen Paul Simonon coming out of the Portuguese café – no one else was looking that handsome in a trilby – and Annie said she'd seen Joe Strummer, but it was just a bloke in a donkey jacket, smoking. Annie, bizarrely, was working in the Body Shop's warehouse. Just her and a few people who came to collect the stock. It would have been back at the very beginning of the company and the products all seemed weird to us. Fruit in soaps? (Fruits that people weren't even eating yet.) We'd never seen that before. Flowers were what soap was meant to smell of, maybe lemons, but not melons and raspberries and guavas – whatever the fuck guava was.

'I remember at the time thinking that Anita Roddick must be off her rocker,' Annie said. 'The woman was obsessed with fruit.' I used to drop into the warehouse a lot as I was living in the nearby Trellick Tower; hopefully there's a statute of limitations on petty pilfering because we made off with a lot of these strange transparent soaps that looked like giant fruit gums.

It was such a lovely afternoon with Annie, and afterwards I walked along Kensington High Street and remembered going to see the film *Christiane F.* with her at the Odeon there. I had cried at the film, and still have a happy-sad cry whenever I hear the song 'Heroes', which was on the soundtrack. I felt genuinely happy. We'd gone to a party in a flat off Kensington Church Street: was that when we were working in the pub together? About 1983? The party was held by an older couple, regulars in the pub, actors, I think. They were loud and drank a lot, and the wife wore 1940s vintage dresses and had a lot of 'anecdotes'; he wore cream linen suits and smoked liquorice Rizla roll-ups. The flat belonged to an aunt. There seemed to be a lot of people who had vague relatives who owned flats in London then. The main reason I remember the party is that I did the classic of walking around with my skirt accidentally tucked into my knickers.

Looking at new summer clothes in the shop windows as I walked along, I made a note of any she would like. We always talked about clothes – not in a following-fashion serious way but in a what- or who-we-wanted-to-look-like way. Annie wanted to look like 'a war correspondent on their day off' – casual cottons but not in a 'mumsie White Stuff way'. We loved a rant about shops we didn't like: White Stuff, Joules and JoJo Maman Bébé. Especially JoJo Maman Bébé. One day we were going to run in there and just shout, 'Go fuck yourself, Jojo, and your bébé!'

'Like the lion lady in *Born Free* but not as English, that's how I'd like to dress – like the lion lady but Italian,' Annie said once. Which led to a long conversation about how the lion lady could never have been Italian because, according to Annie, 'Italians don't like animals. That's why no one in Italy has pets. Have you ever seen a dog on a lead in Rome?'

'Yes, loads,' I replied.

Annie often made statements like that. She would declare something absolutely ludicrous as a fact, with utter conviction, just to see how much you would believe, for her own entertainment.

'You're taking nonsense, dear,' I said.

Annie at the Ribat of Monastir in Tunisia,
in her favourite Kate Adie 'lady traveller' gear.

15

The Worst of Times

Then everything got confusing. I didn't know what much of it meant, but I did know that Annie was having more seizures, fits that were frightening for Martin to deal with. She had to be taken to hospital by ambulance several times.

She went back into Charing Cross for another operation. I was there when she woke up. She was upset and distressed and tried to pull out the tubes in her arm, saying, 'I'm never going to get well.' That phrase was like a knife in my heart. Martin tried to soothe her. She looked at me like she didn't know me. I suddenly felt scared and guilty. I was smiling at her but I felt like an animal smiling to show I was not a threat, to show that I was on her side.

I'm ashamed to say I left. I think I said something to Martin along the lines of there being no point in my being around, that I wasn't helping, but there was a look in her eyes: she didn't want me there.

It was fear in her eyes, raw fear. She was afraid, and I was afraid of her fear. It seems unbelievable now that I left, but if I'm truly honest, I thought she would turn on me. It was a justified fear; she had turned on me periodically throughout our lives. She needed to lash out, and I should have let her, but I ran away.

She cancelled seeing me whenever we arranged to meet. I couldn't find any more 'fun' cards to send. I traipsed into every card shop I saw, but nothing was suitable any more. It felt like I was in a weird vacuum – what was this stage of cancer?

I was doing the Edinburgh Festival and we had long talks on the phone. We didn't usually have long talks on the phone. I know now that she was on really strong doses of steroids and 'uppers' so she would talk for hours, kind of raving but fun.

Then the emails got weird. Some were almost stream-of-consciousness stuff. Some were really nasty – those ones were like a gut punch, mean and vicious, tearing me apart – saying that I didn't really care about her. How could she still not know how much I loved her? How was I still salt in her wounds?

I sat sobbing over one email and my husband said, 'She's angry, she doesn't mean it. I'd be angry and lash out, too, if I was her.' Of course, of course she was angry. She was lashing out at Martin, too. The fear was lashing out. Then I realised how silly I was being. What did my feelings matter? I didn't have cancer.

Then, out of the blue and two weeks early, she sent me three ridiculously funny cards for my birthday. The writing was shaky and almost illegible; I stared at it for ages, scared by the look of it.

Then an email came from Martin.

From: Martin

To: Jo Caulfield, James Caulfield

Sent: 14 September 2016

Subject: Annie

Dear James and Jo,

I am sorry to be writing to you like this but I have been think-ing about it a lot and I feel that I need to fully update you on Annie's condition. It is not good.

I wish I could speak to you both in person rather than by email but this was the only way I could think to lay everything out plainly for both of you.

I hope you will understand when I say please don't tell Annie I am emailing you as it would upset her right now, and she is very easily upset.

Annie is now three weeks past her treatment of head radi-otherapy. All her hair has fallen out, which they told us would be a possibility. More serious is that she now has a large protuberance on the top of her head where the lesion was removed in January. I think this is the new growth and it is, we were told back last month, inoperable.

We are going back into the Marsden where the radiother-apy was carried out next Tuesday for them to give Annie a check up but I don't think the prognosis is good.

We were in to see her lung oncologist on Monday, Dr Tom at Chelsea and Westminster. He has always been honest with us.

He examined Annie and her head and was not positive about our next options.

I think he was laying the groundwork for us to hear that the options of further treatment are going to be severely limited. Annie now has a serious cough and some difficulty breathing at times, which he thinks might be a recurrence of her lung cancer. We go for a new X-ray on Friday.

He is saying in her present very weakened condition he could not consider any further chemotherapy.

It might be that Dr Fiona, the brain specialist at the Marsden, might consider more radiotherapy on Annie's head but it is a very punishing tool. Partial head radiotherapy, which is what she got back in February, is not an option anymore.

In terms of Annie's general condition, she has been severely weakened ever since the series of seizures she had. She has not had any seizures for three to four months but she still has trouble walking by herself or going very far. Her left leg drags and doing up buttons on her shirt is beyond her most days.

The hoped for improvements and return to physical well-being has not happened. In the last few weeks she has not been writing or reading books because she does not have the energy or focus to do so. This is so unlike Annie, as you both know.

Our GP has referred us to the local hospice and we are waiting to see what help they can offer us; maybe have a carer come in once or twice a week to help out or look after her. At the moment I don't like to leave her alone for more than the time it takes me to go to the shops for provisions. Her friend Sarah has come in and sat with Annie a few times but it is difficult to ask friends to come in as Annie does not like people seeing her like this.

I have been trying to keep positive for Annie and for yourselves and her friends but I think we are coming to a time when we need to be more honest.

Annie's immediate response after seeing Dr Tom on Monday is to keep up a positive front in front of family and friends, so I am going behind her back by talking to you like this, and that is why I would ask you to be careful in what you say to her.

Next week we see Dr Fiona and hear what she says about Annie's response to the latest treatment and what she can offer for Annie next. But the indications I am getting is that we are now getting nearer to the palliative care stage.

I don't know if I am doing right by talking to you about this. I feel I should be telling you the full truth. I feel I need to prepare you for that and also I think you two need to have a talk between yourselves about your mother and what you tell her. I am thinking if Annie is put into a palliative care position then do we tell your mother so she can at least have a chance to come down and say goodbye.

After next Tuesday's meeting with Dr Fiona, I will let you know the update.

I am so sorry to be writing an email like this.

Martin

I now know that what we had gone through up until this point was 'cancer, the good times'. The chemo, the radiotherapy, the operations – that's not the worst part. The worst part is when they tell you that they can't give you any more treatment because your body can't take it.

I can't imagine how awful it was for Martin to have been so alone during this.

Annie's pride, her wanting so much not to be pitied – I am my sister's sister, I understand her feelings, her need to cling on to hope and dignity. In wildlife documentaries they often talk about animals dragging themselves off to die alone, away from the herd. I had always thought it sounded noble and dignified, but seeing people dying of cancer, I realised why they wanted to die alone; they know they're weak and vulnerable and the other animals could hurt them. That's what my sister was doing; she was trying to protect herself. She was withdrawing into herself. If she'd had a shell or a burrow, she would have crawled into it and stayed there.

She was so scared, so sensitive, so vulnerable. Terrified of someone saying out loud, 'You're dying of cancer.' She was right: why should she have to deal with that? She needed to manage her feelings on her own terms, to peek at the possible outcome every now and again.

It was her cancer.

16

'It's going to be a bumpy night . . .'

Bette Davis in *All About Eve*.

I went straight down to London and met Martin at the Chelsea and Westminster Hospital.

'What's *she* doing here?' Annie demanded, glaring at me. She didn't look like herself. Her face seemed huge, all puffed up from steroids; she looked like an angry football. There was a doctor in her room, and he was saying stuff like 'so we'll just keep her comfortable' and 'try and get some physio, get some movement' and using words like 'palliative care'.

'She's your sister and she loves you,' Martin said. I wanted to run away again. What the fuck was going on?

'Does she know?' Annie said.

'Yes,' said Martin.

I didn't really, though; I didn't even know what there was to know. Why was this doctor looking at me with such sympathy?

Looking back, that tiny exchange was one of the very few times that Annie acknowledged anything about the situation in front of me.

'Does she *know*?'

'Yes.'

She retracted her claws, relaxed back in the bed and humphed.

A humph from Annie was a good thing. It was self-deprecating, mocking her own bad humour, and it meant, 'Well, I'm not happy about that, but okay, just watch yourself.'

Then there were a couple of noisy fun days. Annie being charming and hilarious and totally engaged in the big red chair at the Chelsea and Westminster. If you've never seen one of these chairs before, it's a bit like Captain Kirk's chair in *Star Trek*. Annie was lifted into one of these chairs, which they then wheeled into a day room as if she were a queen in her throne room ready to receive visitors. And like a queen she gave a brilliant performance of a well and happy person.

And she had so many visitors. Aunties, uncles and cousins, the loud, funny Northern Irish voices that Annie loved, filled the room, as well as James, Mum and me and Annie's closest friends, Woodrow and Sarah.

Woodrow brought in one of those adult Ladybird books, a parody of the *Janet and John* books we'd had as kids in the sixties. Instead of picking apples in the orchard, Janet gives John a blowjob (I think there was a lot of fingering too), and I just remember my mum's look of complete incomprehension.

At one point Annie's catheter bag split and started to leak all over the floor. I panicked, thinking this was the most humiliating thing that could ever happen to someone in a roomful of people. Your wee is spreading in a pool beneath your chair and everyone's just chatting on. I rushed to get someone to change it. I never know what the hierarchy is in hospitals. I knew that nurses didn't clean up stuff, but I also knew that an orderly couldn't change the catheter bag – and were they even called orderlies? If you're asking someone to clean up urine, I think you should be pretty sure that it's in their job description, but then, if it is your job it's probably annoying to have middle-class wankers like me being overly apologetic about it.

But the orderly/nurse/cleaner/porter/patient/random visitor/ consultant who I asked for help didn't come and sort it out. Annie didn't seem bothered, though; she just laughed. Six months earlier she'd kicked up a fuss in the hospital and refused to even have a catheter. She was adamant about it: 'Jo, I will not sit with a bag of wee next to my head.' Now it didn't matter to her. It was a boundary crossed. What she had seen as undignified then was a necessity now and she was absolutely fine with it. Because she had to be.

Then we heard that her Macmillan nurse had found a place for her in a hospice and she was to be moved there. Annie never called it a hospice; she called it a 'halfway house', sometimes even referring to it as a 'sort of spa'. She said she was there to do some physio which would help get her walking again and then, when she was stronger, she'd go home and start more chemo. That was her story. Dr Tom had agreed with Martin to say to Annie that, if she got stronger, she would get more treatment. She needed hope. The 'halfway house sort of spa' was completely her invention.

One day I was walking to the Tube from the hospice and I bumped into Martin, who was going in to see Annie. It was nice to see him, and I joked that Annie had been a bit grumpy that day and I didn't seem to be able to do anything right. Martin laughed and then said, 'Well, she's dying.' I did a sort of mental double take. Why would he say that? I don't think I had heard anyone actually say that she was dying. As far as I was concerned, she wasn't dying, and I thought it was kind of rude of Martin to say that. You don't just say out loud in the street, 'Oh, your sister's dying.' I thought it was a very odd thing for him to say, especially because he's one of the kindest people I know. Why on earth would he go around saying casually that Annie was dying? It's like I hadn't fully made the connection that people who leave a hospice leave because they have died; somehow I thought they had just . . . gone home. Was there ever anyone so stupid as me? James and I hadn't talked about her dying. I know now that he thought I knew. But I really didn't. People would say, 'Well, you were in denial.' I don't think I was. I just thought someone like Annie wouldn't die. She was too important, too essential to my life. It was the sort of thing that happened to other people, people I didn't know. She was too special and . . . she wouldn't want to die, she wouldn't allow it.

Annie really loved her room at the Royal Trinity Hospice. I had imagined cold magnolia walls and Victorian iron beds, but it's the most beautiful place. Everything's bright, modern and sort of Scandinavian-looking, and her room had French doors that opened onto her own private terrace with views over the peaceful, lush gardens. And it was free! I can't think what we would've done without it.

Visitors could come and go as they liked, there were no rules, and you could nip out to the kitchen and make a cup of tea any time you fancied. Tea-making was a very good way of getting people in and out of the room. If Annie looked pissed off or tired, 'Let's make a cup of tea.' If you needed to speak to someone privately away from Annie, 'Let's make a cup of tea.' If you needed to get out of the room because you suddenly realised you were upset, 'Let's make a cup of tea.'

And she needed every sort of care. It was only when she asked me to move the blanket over her feet and I lifted her legs that I realised she couldn't walk. Her legs were dead weights; she couldn't move them at all. I don't understand how lung cancer can do that to your body. How it can take it over completely. All she could move was her head and arms. It had truly spread everywhere, yet she wasn't a feeble little stick lying in the bed wasting away. She looked big and strong, she was eating well and her voice wasn't weak. She never seemed short of breath and her life force was so strong that she never really seemed ill. She was fooling people far smarter than us. As James said, 'Don't forget she's a good actress, always has been.'

Annie's favourite Hollywood greats were Barbara Stanwyck and Bette Davis, the strong wisecracking women who were complicated and heroic. That's who she was playing. Like the old gentleman she had met when she had her first chemo treatment, she was going to be the best patient.

ANNIE CAULFIELD'S GUILTY PLEASURE

Why I Love *All About Eve*

There's something about the way Bette Davis, with her hands in the pockets of a silk dress, swishes haughtily through this film.

The flash of her eyes and the 'don't mess with me' tilt of her chin are weapons I wish I could conjure when I'm messed with.

Yet despite her magnificence, Bette Davis's character in this film, Margo Channing, is tormented by friends and foes alike, particularly by the conniving minx of the title, Eve Harrington (Anne Baxter).

Margo Channing is a grande-dame of Broadway but she's forty, playing twenty-four, and Bill Sampson, the love of her life, is only thirty-two: 'Bill's thirty-two, he looks thirty-two. He looked it five years ago. He'll look it twenty years from now.'

At this vulnerable juncture, with Margo's closest friends growing tired of her temperament, wide-eyed Eve Harrington insinuates herself into Margo's life. Eve makes herself indispensable while she goes after Margo's career, man, friendships …

The storms this provokes lead to some of the most quotable lines in cinema. We all know, 'Fasten your seatbelts. It's going to be a bumpy night,' or the introduction of a young Marilyn Monroe's character as being from the 'Copacabana School of Dramatic Art'. This is uttered by the compellingly wicked theatre critic, Addison DeWitt, played by sardonic, sinister George Sanders, who twists and observes events with amused detachment.

Some of the best lines though, are from Margo's ex-vaudevillian dresser, Birdie, played by the indomitable Thelma

Ritter. When observing a pile of fur coats on the bed at a fancy party, she remarks, 'The bed looks like a dead animal act.' And when Eve tells everyone her heartbreaking backstory, Birdie mutters, 'What a story. Everything but the bloodhounds snappin' at her rear end.'

Streetwise Birdie is the first to spot Eve as phoney. But will Eve get her comeuppance?

Not really. Eve gets fame and fortune but at a terrible price. Does Margo win? Well, according to the intentions of this 1950 Joseph L. Mankiewicz film, she does. Much as I love this film, there's a moment in it when my heart sinks. It's like the moment in *Calamity Jane* where Doris Day puts on a dress and you know she won't be her wonderful self any more.

Margo Channing doesn't care about Eve's success because she has domestic bliss instead: 'In the last analysis, nothing is any good unless you can look up just before dinner, or turn around in bed — and there he is. Without that, you're not a woman.'

So perhaps the message makes *All About Eve* something of a guilty pleasure. However, even if you hate the message, you'll stay for the wisecracking dialogue, emotional tension and great storming, furniture-chewing confrontations.

I know if I've had a bumpy night of my own, *All About Eve* will be my comfort food. I'll hug a cushion and puzzle for the umpteenth time over Margo Channing's bizarrely effective, unfathomable put-down: 'Remind me to tell you about when I looked into the heart of an artichoke.' The day I get to use that in a non-greengrocery context, my life will be complete.

The first time I went to visit her in the hospice, Sarah and I wheeled her out into the sun on her big bed. A young nurse (who Annie liked because she always came in with a hangover and a story to tell) said that we should be careful because Stephen Hawking's nurse tried to kill him by wheeling him out into the sun and leaving him there. That really tickled Annie, and then as we tried to steer her bed back inside before she got sunstroke, Sarah (who is five foot nothing) somehow got dragged under the bed. We were all laughing, but I remember panicking because I couldn't steer the bed in a straight line and it kept knocking into the door. You know that way where you laugh so much you have no strength? It was a bizarrely lovely moment.

'When did you last really laugh?'

'Whacking my dying sister's bed repeatedly into a door.'

Annie enjoyed herself telling Sarah what a terrible driver I am, which I freely admit is true, although not in a daredevil way – no, I'm a bad driver in a dangerously slow pensioner way. The fast lane on the motorway? I've never been in it. If there's roadworks on the motorway, my husband always says, 'Oh, look, Jo, you'll like this. There's roadworks ahead – you can slow down.'

She told Sarah about us going on holiday to Sardinia, Annie, Adam and me. They wanted to hire mopeds to explore the mountainous countryside. I did not think this was a good idea. I'd never seen so many people with broken arms and legs as in Sardinia, and all those injuries were from motorbike accidents. Annie and Adam would zoom off fearlessly and then have to wait for me to catch up; I would eventually come tootling along at what I considered a safe speed.

One afternoon we stopped at some spot of great natural beauty, where the car park was packed with coaches and tourists, a good-sized audience to witness me humiliating myself.

On mopeds in Sardinia, Annie checking out an
even more dangerous route through her binoculars.
Look closely, and you can see my white knuckles
gripping the handlebars.

As I started the bike I somehow got the accelerator stuck on
full rev but still had the brake on, so the bike rose up into the
air. I clung on and was tossed around the car park like I was
riding a bucking bronco. I remember being in fear of my life,
yet I could see Adam and Annie weak with laughter as I repeatedly whizzed past them on one wheel, screaming my head off.

One word that we used over and over again in the hospice was 'appropriate'. Annie would say people's behaviour
was either 'appropriate' or 'inappropriate'. When people were
inappropriate they would upset her, anger her, bore her or in
some way displease her, and you could be taken off the visitor
list for inappropriate behaviour.

Once, Annie was outraged that a volunteer was wearing a
mustard dress. 'A mustard-coloured dress? Doesn't she know

133

there're people here with cancer? Upsetting us all with her nasty dress.' She was joking, but it was based on something very important. It took all of Annie's energy to try to seem well (not *get* well any more, just *seem* well), so she couldn't waste precious time and effort on things or people that upset her.

The mustard-dress remark was Annie being funny. It's the sort of thing that's difficult to convey on paper. I hope you are getting a sense of her: she was both acerbic and adorable at the same time and always ready to laugh at herself.

Once, we were in a seaside café in Ramsgate, one of those Italian ice-cream parlours that do proper coffee. Annie ordered an espresso and the young woman behind the counter said, 'That's the really strong small cup of coffee, just so you know.' Annie could not have been more offended. 'Yes, thank you, I know what an espresso is,' she retorted before flouncing off. I pointed out that a lot of people in Ramsgate probably didn't know what an espresso was. I then did an impression of her 'I know what an espresso is' face, and she cackled with glee at her own ridiculousness. After that, if I pointed out she had her 'espresso face' on, she would always laugh.

Making her laugh was always something I got a thrill out of. Some people in life just bring out the funny in you. Annie always did. I would almost think up routines for her, and sometimes I wonder if that's why I was drawn to stand-up comedy. When I did my first-ever gig, that thrill of the audience laughing was familiar and comforting (okay, they didn't laugh a lot at my first gig, but there *were* laughs). It felt immediately as if I'd found the thing I should be doing in life, and not before time – I was fast becoming the oldest waitress in town.

I'm embarrassed to write this, but at about this time I sent Annie an email saying how much she meant to me. It was very much the sort of email you would send to someone if they were dying. What was I thinking? I'd seen it in films, I suppose, and I'd never been in this situation, so it seemed like a good thing to do.

She was furious, and I totally get why. I wouldn't have done that normally. It was selfish: always think about whether you're doing something to make yourself feel better or to try and make the other feel better, because that email did *not* make Annie feel better. By not going along with her narrative, I had committed the worst kind of betrayal.

As a family we made mistakes. One day we were all gathered round the bed, the whole family together. We are not that kind of family, and I suddenly saw it from Annie's point of view; we'd unwittingly created what must have looked to her like a deathbed scene. After that we coordinated our visits so we weren't a depressing family group gathered at the end of her bed. I always texted Martin to check if it was okay to visit in case Annie was tired and had had a lot of visitors already that day (in which case one more wouldn't be helpful). Just because someone is ill doesn't mean we should forget our manners; let them keep some control over their own life. I wouldn't have dropped in on Annie without asking before she was ill, so why do it now? Being ill doesn't mean a loss of your right to privacy. You shouldn't lose the right to choose who you see and how you spend your time. If you're already feeling vulnerable, people shouldn't expect you to have an open-door policy whereby just anyone can march into your room and intrude when you are at your most fragile and delicate. Try to be a good visitor.

Bring something to the party and don't sit there with a bloody hangdog face like a spectre at the feast.

My brother took on the job of bringing Mum down from Melton Mowbray. She was never quite herself after my dad died; she needed James's help. London was too big and busy for her and, unusually, she complained about everything. Maybe that was her way of coping, but the station was too cold, the train was too hot, the platform was too long and the taxi was too bumpy. For my mum, who had always been so stoic, who had packed up a dozen homes in the Air Force, and always made the best of things, finally it was too much. Losing her husband and now her daughter, everything was simply too unbearable to face. Maybe it was better to distract herself by complaining about what was happening right in front of her. I know this meant that James didn't get time alone with Annie, time to really say goodbye, not by saying goodbye obviously but just talking about stuff, trips they'd done together. I know he misses that time that he didn't get to spend with his sister, and I will always be grateful. He told me later that from quite early on he'd known Annie wasn't getting better. He said he was worried she would see it in his eyes and so he kept his distance. What a truly unselfish and loving thing to do.

Annie got distressed one day and said to me, 'Joey, I don't want loads of people coming here. I just want to be with Martin and be normal and watch my box sets.' It was so simple it was heartbreaking.

17

Catholic Dogs and Morphine

It was in the hospice that I got to know Sarah. She was always full of fun and chat. Sometimes it could be awkward, and people wouldn't know what to say, but Sarah always seemed to relax everyone.

Annie didn't want to talk much about the outside world once she was in the hospice. Not in a depressed way, but because she had created a world of characters and running jokes in this new world of hers. She no longer cared about news or current affairs – I suppose your worldview is different and those things just become unimportant. But she did become fixated on a few things. One was about acts of kindness, about how she'd given a sandwich to a Romanian man who was selling *The Big Issue* and they'd had a lovely conversation and made a connection. Martin would come in and I'd say, 'She's talking about that bloody Romanian man again.' (No offence, Romanian man, but it did get a bit tedious.)

The other thing was in a similar vein; it was about wanting your life to have mattered. She said that there was a Jewish allegory about a tapestry – the world was like a tapestry and that everyone should aim to add a few stitches to the cloth to help finish it. She was being perfectly serious and genuine when she spoke about this. She wanted to have put a stitch in the tapestry.

She was adapting in all sorts of ways and making plans for when she came out of the hospice. She'd say things like, 'I won't be able to go on big travels any more, but I can do little trips. Woodrow and I are going to Legoland, and Sarah and I are going to Strabane.'

If you know Strabane, then you know it's generally not a place where people want to go. It's a place you go to visit relatives or you don't go to at all. It's on the border of County Tyrone, in Northern Ireland. Mum grew up in the countryside there. It's a town wrecked by the Troubles. The whole centre has gone, and in the eighties it was mentioned on the news a lot, usually prefaced with phrases like 'largely Nationalist Strabane'. Mum's memories of Strabane are of a prosperous market town in the forties with a very fancy department store, Wellworths, and a ladies' clothing shop that she and Granny went to, Miss Jones of Strabane. Annie wrote a radio play about Strabane's most famous son, the writer Flann O'Brien, and spent time there doing research. She enjoyed the directness of the locals, most of whom advised her that no one was very interested in Flann O'Brien. 'Good of you though it is to be interested in him yourself,' said the owner of her B&B.

In the hospice she had started telling Sarah about Strabane, how they would buy an old house there and write books and grow cheese. It was a plan made on morphine, but it seemed to make Annie happy; plans for the future were a good thing, so Sarah became our Strabane estate agent and brought in details of land and houses for sale.

Annie asked me to think of somewhere we could go together on our trip. I chose Ruislip Lido. We had a lovely couple of hours that afternoon planning our trip and reminiscing. I hadn't been there since we were kids when we lived at RAF Hendon. I think we only went there a couple of times as kids, but it made a big impression on me. I really liked the fact that there was grass around the swimming pool. You could sit on the grass and then run into the pool — no hard, slippy tiles like at the swimming baths. What more could a child want? I also liked the fact that it was really busy. My dad seemed to have a horror of busy places. When we went to the beach we always had to walk for miles across the sand dunes like a Lawrence of Arabia tribute act. We'd carry all our belongings past all the normal families until we got to the most remote part of the beach. Often there was a reason that that part of the beach was empty — a reason like rip currents or, as in the time we nearly lost James, a lagoon that would rapidly be swallowed by the North Sea as the tide came in.

As a kid I thought that Ruislip Lido was working-class, and while I wasn't quite sure what that was, it seemed to be a good thing. It seemed to be more relaxed. These people did things that we didn't do; they shouted a lot, had caravan holidays, went to Butlin's, wore fashionable clothes and ate hotdogs and funfair food. They were more casual and less worried about 'doing the wrong thing'.

There must have been some fire regulations at the lido, because my father didn't bring along a Primus stove and a saucepan like he did at the seaside. He would heat up tinned stew in a saucepan and we'd have mashed potato that had been kept warm in a thermos flask. How do you get mashed potato out of a thermos flask? you might ask. With great difficulty. But because Ruislip Council didn't want to start the second Fire of London, we got the rare treat of having sandwiches and crisps.

We chatted about family history, telling stories we'd shared before, stories that were always interesting and comforting. It's a simple pleasure that never gets boring because each time you have the 'family history conversation' you're always hopeful of learning a new bit of information. My brother is the oracle on family history; these conversations always included a lot of 'Well, James says . . .' Maybe it's because he's a priest and people confess to him – or maybe he's just a terrible gossip.

It was a good afternoon.

People casually say, 'Oh, when I can't feed myself and some-one has to wipe my bum, just pull the plug. What kind of life is that?' How foolish and wasteful. Annie would have taken any kind of life she could get.

Life may get very small, but a big person can do a lot with it. That's sailing very close to some sort of hideous inspirational quote, but it's true. Annie had her brain and her voice, and she could enjoy the people she loved. That's huge. She would have been so able to live like that. Limited though it was, she would have taken it and been happy. She would have been her bad-tempered, funny, grumpy self as well; God forbid that cancer made her nicer or less herself. But she wanted to live, she wanted to live so much. She had much more she wanted to write, so many more days of just being quietly happy with Martin. She hadn't finished yet.

One afternoon when I went to visit her she was lying in the dark with the curtains drawn and the door closed. The nurse explained that they'd given her a suppository and they were waiting for it to work. She said to wait outside. I sat outside her room and cried. The floodgates opened, and I couldn't stop crying. It just seemed the saddest, loneliest place in the world for Annie to be, lying there in the dark, completely helpless. Poor Annie, that this was what cancer had done to her, to my amazing sister who I loved so much.

A man came up (a nurse, I think) and asked if I was okay. I'd seen him before; he'd been sitting with a woman with short dark hair who was crying. She had that just-grown-back hair-cut. The crying woman had said, 'I just want to get well,' and I'd thought, 'Well, you will get well because you've had chemo.' When I thought about her later, after I'd been visiting the hospice more, it hit me. She wasn't going to get well.

'Are you okay?' I remember clearly thinking, 'No, I'm not, but talking to you won't help.' What was I going to say? We're in a hospice; it's a variation on the same terrible story. It's worth knowing that sometimes talking doesn't help, sometimes people just want to sit and cry. It was kind of him to offer, but I was also grateful that he just left me in the corridor to unself-consciously cry my eyes out.

I was still on tour, so I'd been up north and had missed some days. Days in which she had changed. She was deteriorating. The morphine dose had gone up, but I didn't realise the implication; I had never been around someone in this condition before. Annie just seemed to be rambling and talking rubbish. She repeated the same nonsense and started laughing. Martin laughed as well and agreed with her. For the first time I thought, 'Where's Annie?'

'Just go with it,' Martin said. Again, that was great advice: don't try to wrestle a person on morphine back into the real world. Go with them, go into their wonderful world and let them show you around.

And it *was* still Annie, it was just Annie on morphine. She was doing what she'd always done; she was playing with words, having fun with them. Nothing could be more quintessentially Annie than that. And she knew she was being funny. She enjoyed the sound of certain words and would repeat things over and over. I'd been listening to George Clinton and for some reason I started singing 'who's got the funk'. Something in that obviously appealed to her and we invented a song about Doctor Funkenstein and trousers – just funny-sounding words and nonsense. Annie chuckled gleefully. She was still herself.

She liked to have the door to her room open so she could see all the comings and goings and we could pass judgement and make up stories about all the other patients and staff.

One afternoon someone from the hospice came in with a book for Annie. The only way I can describe it is to say it was like a Baby's First Year book, and the idea was for patients to fill in things about themselves and their lives. The woman wanted to fill it in with Annie, so was asking her questions. She managed one question before I jumped in and stopped her. She'd asked Annie, 'What did you used to be?'

It sent a chill right through me. Annie didn't 'used to be', she still *is* a writer. And anyway, you're always a writer. Oddly, Annie wasn't at all put out by the question. In the end Martin and I had to manhandle the book away from her. 'But it's about *me* – they want to know about *me*, Martin.' She was an adorable egomaniac up to the end.

We'd started having little evenings in with Annie. Friends would bring in wine and we'd all just chat and laugh, and the staff didn't mind how rowdy we were. They said it was nice to hear some loud happy voices. Annie loved it. I was sitting with her one Sunday afternoon and a dog went past the door. She pointed and laughed, 'Ha! A dog!'

'Must be visiting afternoon for dogs,' I said.

'Dog day afternoon . . . dog day afternoon, Joey!' she cackled happily, and we had a long conversation about whether dogs should be allowed wine.

'Not on a Sunday,' Annie decided. 'I don't think dogs can have wine on a Sunday, not if they're Catholic.'

'Is the dog Catholic, Annie?'

'Looks it to me. Yes! Ha! Yes.' She seemed delighted with this thought. 'We'll ask James,' she said. 'Ask James – he'll know.'

It was gloriously freeing to just go with these flights of morphine-induced fancy. To be slightly nuts. It released all the pressure, to be totally in the moment with her, not thinking about anything but those thoughts of dogs and wine. It kind of made sense anyway: there was a dog in the hospice, we had been having wine and James is a priest, so of course he'd know if Catholic dogs were allowed wine on a Sunday. And *Dog Day Afternoon* is a great film.

It's so important to remember to enjoy the person while you have them. I'm grateful to my brain; it didn't let me process what was happening. If I had, I wouldn't have all these memories. I would just have been sad and bawling my eyes out at the end of her bed, wasting these precious last days. I think mine protected me. It knows me better than I know myself. It let me enjoy her.

One of my sweetest memories is of feeding her soup. It's a small moment, but to be able to laugh with your big sister as you try to get pea soup in her mouth is worth being alive for. And she bloody loved that pea soup. Who knew a person could get so much pleasure from a bowl of soup? It was that life force, that capacity to still have these moments where she was so alive, so seemingly strong, that made it impossible to imagine that she wouldn't get better. Let alone believe that she was dying.

Pea soup and ice cream – I didn't notice that that was all she was eating. The scampi was too difficult now.

18

A Fierce Girl

'Fuck me, it's Sister Theresa!' Luckily I didn't say that out loud when I saw her sitting by Annie's bed, large as life. Sister Theresa had taught history at the convent, and I hadn't seen her for forty years. Like most adults you knew as a child she wasn't as old as I'd thought she was. She seemed to be in her late sixties now and she'd seemed in her late sixties forty years ago. She and Annie had had a real connection and kept in touch, so I understood why she was there, but it was so weird to see her sitting in what Annie and I called 'off-duty nun clothes'. Nuns don't wear habits any more, but you can still spot them. They favour browns and navies, an M&S button-up cardie, a certain type of sensible sandal worn with tan tights and the classic seventies lesbian short haircut.

When I first went to school she was called Mother Theresa, but something happened in the late seventies and the nuns went all hippie-ish and egalitarian. 'Hey, no hierarchy here, man. We're all just sisters – everyone's equal.' It seemed a shame for some of the really old nuns, especially the 'kitchen nuns' like Mother Veronica. Mother Veronica wasn't a trained teacher; she was probably someone whose family had decided they'd have one less mouth to feed if they sent her off to England to become a nun. She was always kind and gave us toffees from her Tardis-like apron pocket. She did all the hard work in the kitchen and the laundry, and then when she finally got a bit of status and a title, after all those years of grunt work, they took it away from her.

Back to Sister Theresa, though. At first I didn't understand the surge of love that I was suddenly feeling for this nun (she had terrified me at school). Then I realised: she loved Annie and she had come to see her. She was here when it mattered.

Annie and Sister Theresa had had stand-up rows at school (you really didn't do that then – argue with a nun). One night Annie had shouted at her in the chapel corridor. People talked about it for months. It was very dramatic. My best friend Sally was expelled from school. She hadn't done anything particularly wrong; we were just 'naughty'. There was so little scope for being bad that we did stupid things, usually involving climbing (trees, sides of buildings and flat roofs were favourites) or sneaking into the nuns' side of the convent. Innocent things, really. But Sally had a sort of confidence about her that nuns didn't like; she didn't play the game. The game was that you did something bad and then you repented; you bowed your head and felt ashamed. That's what I did. Own up, be sorry and then do it again – that's Catholicism in a nutshell. But Sally never appeared to be suitably sorry.

It was a Sunday night, the free time before we went to bed. Sally had been called aside after supper and there were rumours she was in the sun lounge. I can't convey properly all that was implied by the words 'sun lounge', but basically it was a one-way journey. You got called there if someone had died or you were being expelled.

I was trying to find out what was happening to Sally, and people were saying she was definitely in the sun lounge, so I went to find Annie. Annie went up to Sister Theresa, and I think she asked if I could say goodbye to Sally, and then it all kicked off. Sister Theresa said that I was to go into one of the music cells and write an essay on 'what makes a good character'. Because, according to Sister Theresa, I had a 'very bad character'. A prefect walked me to what were called the music cells (tiny rooms with just enough room for a desk and an upright piano). You could say I was sort of under house arrest. I could hear Annie yelling at Sister Theresa, 'How can Jo be bad? She's twelve years old! She's a child!' Annie was also a child; she was sixteen.

About half an hour later Sister Theresa and Annie came to get me and, miracle of miracles, Sister Theresa sort of apologised! She said that she had only wanted to keep me away from the sun lounge while Sally packed and left the school.

Now, Sister Theresa was sitting at Annie's bedside. She had
brought with her a copy of a poem that Annie had written for
her when she was at school. I had never known about this.
Only my mum had a copy. Sister Teresa said she still had the
original, that she'd kept it for over forty-five years.

Annie really admired Sister Theresa; she thought she'd led
an interesting and useful life. She'd been a nun at the UN and
lived in New York. She was like a supernun, travelling the
world as a sort of nun ambassador and now doing work with
addicts and homeless people.

Sister Theresa said there was always one child you taught
who you never forgot, who was special. For her it was Annie.
'It was her intelligence,' Sister Theresa said. 'Such intelligence
and bravery. A fierce girl.'

What a great description. It makes me smile to think how
much Annie would've loved it. I think the Irish use of fierce is
exactly right here. A fierce girl. What a magnificent thing to
be.

A couple of days before she died I told the doctor that Annie
hadn't eaten anything. I remember rattling on about how much
she liked ice cream and that she wasn't even eating ice cream. I
thought they'd find a way to feed her through a drip or something. Has anyone ever been so dumb? I still didn't get it. I
thought they were keeping her alive, not helping her to die.

The doctor said, 'That's what happens. It's the body shutting
down.' There were a million signals forewarning me that she
was dying, but I just couldn't process them. It wasn't her time;
neither of us were ready.

Annie slept more and more, waking only for brief moments,
but even then I don't know how conscious she was. Her eyes

would roll back in her head and then she would fall asleep again. Martin left me alone with her, to give us some privacy. It felt like an out-of-body experience, me stroking her hand and telling her what a good big sister she'd been. Part of me knew that I would want to have done this, part of me was just watching, wondering why I was doing it. But I also thought, 'This is for me. It's doing nothing for her. There's nothing that I *can* do for her.'

She was high as a kite on morphine, so I'm ninety-nine per cent sure she was unaware of what I said, but who knows? And it did make me feel better. I can still feel the soft texture of her skin, and remember the look of her hands, so different to mine. I have long bony hands like my mum; Annie's are rounder, with strong nails.

I got home to Edinburgh on the Sunday, having seen Annie every day that I was in London. It seems so weird now; I was playing the Comedy Store at night and visiting my sister in the hospice in the day. But that's what we all have to do, isn't it? Carry on. As soon as I got home I said to my husband, 'I don't think she's got much longer.' When I said that I felt like someone acting in a drama. He agreed that I should go back immediately. I went back down to London again the next day.

There were about six of us in her room. My mum and my brother had been in in the afternoon, but now it was just Martin, Annie's oldest friends and me. We sat in her room talking and laughing and having paper cups of wine. Her friend Bev had come over from Spain; she kept rubbing Annie's arm and then holding her hand. I thought how nice that was, how important it is to be touched.

Every now and again Annie would make a noise as though she was part of the conversation. We were being silly and having a laugh, which she would have thought was very 'appropriate' and we were talking about *her*, which she would've thought absolutely appropriate.

I hope it was nice, to drift off to the noise of people who love you, with one of us always holding her hand or stroking her arm.

Martin got a call an hour after we left. Annie died just after one o'clock in the morning. She had asked for this quote by Michel de Montaigne to be read at her funeral: 'If you don't know how to die, don't worry; Nature will tell you what to do on the spot, fully and adequately. She will do this job perfectly for you; don't bother your head about it.' And it was: just a moment, nothing dramatic.

I haven't much to say about how I felt at the time, because in my brain her death hadn't happened yet. My mum and brother and I were all pleased (or perhaps comforted) that we had all spent time with her on her last day. I didn't know what it was like to be without her yet. Some people say they feel numb after someone dies, and I think I did feel kind of numb, but it was combined with a sick feeling in my stomach. It was like the feeling I would get as a kid when I had to go back to boarding school – a sick, fearful feeling. The fear of what's coming.

19

Giving Her a Wonderful Day

Annie in County Donegal, 2010.

When someone dies in a film people often fling themselves onto the furniture and start weeping and wailing. I didn't cry. There were things to be done, arrangements to be made and Martin would need help.

A nurse from the hospice talked to us. She told us the official cause of death was lung cancer. It still seems weird; Annie wasn't on a ventilator, and she could breathe on her own right up until she died.

Then we somehow got into a conversation about Ubers. Martin said he didn't know what he would've done without

Uber and what a godsend cheap cabs had been. The nurse's dad was a black cab driver – a fact that she mentioned several times with increasing annoyance – but Martin was completely oblivious and, in his grief-demented way, talked more and more about the wonder of Ubers. I remember thinking how surreal it was: my sister's just died and we seem to be getting into a row about cabs with this lovely nurse.

The next thing that had to happen was the funeral. We wanted to give her a really great day. A funeral is such a clever invention, so necessary; it lets you pour all your love into that day. It's something to cherish in the future and it feels like you've extended your time with them by creating this extra day.

It's much better that funerals can be so personal and informal these days; an eighteen-year-old girl no longer has to have the same dour traditional funeral as an eighty-year-old man. And it's also a fantastic distraction. I don't know how Martin would have got through that first week if he hadn't been running around trying to organise everything and follow Annie's funeral plans to the letter. Ever the dramatist, she had the running order and timings all planned out; she had even included little edit points ('if X overruns, cut the next song').

She wanted a humanist ceremony and to be cremated. The service was to be in Kensal Green Crematorium – there's a nice pub nearby with a big function room. Martin booked everything and got hold of everyone who Annie wanted to speak at the funeral. Famous people (there, I said it) she had worked with and who had become her friends all showed up and made beautiful, funny and moving speeches. Sandi Toksvig was the humanist celebrant. My mum was proud; it's nice to have famous people honour your daughter. It was the worst day, but it was the best day. It's a cliché, and I said it a hundred times that day, but she would've loved it.

It was the best funeral I've ever been to, full of laughter and stories and tears (a good drama needs tears). People clapped after everyone spoke, which I thought was perfect because it just releases the tension and stops there being those awkward silences when everyone just stands about looking stiff and uncomfortable. Woodrow put together a booklet for everyone to keep; it had his thoughts about Annie and lots of photos of her, happy and laughing. Sarah gave a hilarious speech about their first meeting in a BBC writers' room, how Annie had grabbed all the pens for the whiteboard where the storyline ideas were written down, saying, 'If you control the pens, you control the story.' Sarah immediately wanted to be friends with her. She described what a fun and loyal friend Annie had been.

James was allocated ten minutes on Annie's sheet. He did twenty-two, the comic in me unable to turn off my inner timer, and Lenny Henry took the piss out of him for over-running. Hearing the laughter, Lenny looked up to the ceiling and said he was doing what Annie was always telling him to do, going off script and improvising. He talked about how smart and funny she was (they had worked together for over twenty years) and how she should have had more: more success. He was right. She should have had more writing commissioned, more scripts seeing the light of day, more books published, but it's the nature of this beast. Writing is not a fair business. But she left behind an impressive body of work by most writers' standards, and I was grateful to him that he said that, that he appreciated her.

My role was to read a piece from the biography of Norman Lewis (the writer I mentioned earlier that Annie had introduced me to). I was not given a free rein to speak and, I'll be honest, I was pissed off. It was utterly selfish and silly, but it hurt my feelings that she didn't want me to talk. Didn't she trust me? I felt a bit foot-stampy.

I also had to introduce the Maxi Priest song 'Wild World'. She hadn't written what I was to say in that introduction, so I gave myself some leeway. How well she knew me. I read the Norman Lewis piece fine but as soon as I started to go off script, I broke down, just as she knew I would, all those months ago in Charing Cross Hospital when she told me about planning her funeral. She'd said gleefully at the time, 'I've got you introducing Maxi Priest – you'll cry your eyes out.'

In the late eighties, Annie paid for us both to go to The Gambia on holiday. Everywhere we went, that Maxi Priest song seemed to be playing, and we sang it over and over again. Over and over again with the wrong words: 'Oh, baby, baby, it's a *wide* world.' Oh, hang on, that's not it. 'It's a *wild* world . . . Oh . . .'

She was always generous when she had money. Money was sort of communal to Annie; it wasn't important in itself, it was to be shared around. If she had money she'd share it, but when she didn't have any, she expected other people to share theirs with her. I remember she once asked me to lend her the money to pay her tax bill and I suggested that maybe she should put money aside each month like I did so that she'd have the money ready when her tax bill was due. She looked at me in complete horror. What an insane suggestion! It was as though I'd said, 'Do you know how I save? I bury the money in the garden with my own shit.' No, money was not to be saved or thought about; like Mr Micawber, she always believed that something would turn up.

On our holiday to The Gambia, 1986. I'm in my subservient younger-sister position, slightly behind Annie. High-waisted jeans were a thing.

A holiday with Annie was not about relaxing by the pool. I was allowed to do that for one afternoon on our trip to The Gambia – the rest of the time was spent having adventures, travelling around in bush taxis and strange boats upriver. At one point we nearly slept with the same man until we realised that he was going after both of us. He even told us both the same thing: 'I don't really like your sister, I like you.' We couldn't believe he was stupid enough to think we wouldn't confide in each other. We should have played some *Thelma and Louise*-style revenge prank on him, but he was very handsome and there was no reason for us both to miss out, so I took myself out of the running. Well, she was on the planet first.

The song makes me think of crazy taxi journeys and singing in the sunshine. Annie thought the line about finding a lot of nice things to wear was a very lovely thing to wish for someone.

That trip was the beginning of Annie's love for (and fascination with) Africa. She travelled there extensively. She wrote books, radio plays, a radio soap opera for the World Service, worked with a football charity for girls in South Africa when they held the World Cup . . . and even made a documentary in Burkina Faso with Spice Girl Mel B.

She then moved on to Jordan. She'd been crazy about T. E. Lawrence since seeing *Lawrence of Arabia* at the Edgeware Road Odeon as a child. I think the fact that he looked like Peter O'Toole in her head didn't hurt this fascination. She pored over *The Seven Pillars of Wisdom*, Lawrence's bombastic account of his time in Jordan. She made several long trips there and several more after she fell in love with Rathwan, a Bedouin. A very modern Bedouin who drove a taxi. She stayed under the stars in the desert, although it was a little different to Lawrence's time as she said they had a huge generator and a widescreen TV. The book that came out of this, *Kingdom of the Film Stars*, was optioned for a film. It might have actually been made into a film had 9/11 not happened and Hollywood suddenly became uninterested in the story of a sympathetic Muslim man falling in love with a Western woman.

My husband helped Martin get the music together for the funeral. That was quite difficult, as Annie had mostly requested things that didn't exist, such as 'Up On Broadway' when she meant 'Up On The Roof' or (probably) 'On Broadway'. We had to guess which song we thought she was aiming for.

She'd picked a Van Morrison song for Martin (a huge Van fan), but she'd chosen 'Have I Told You Lately', which made Martin laugh as he said no self-respecting Van fan would ever choose that song; she may as well have picked Chris Rea's

'Driving Home For Christmas' if she wanted to make him look like he had terrible taste in music.

But she knew us all so well. She had written in her plans that 'Martin is to write something, but he probably won't be capable of reading so he should give it to Mike to read'. It was so funny how she was directing and controlling the narrative even after her death – bossing us about one last time. Mike, an old friend, read Martin's words beautifully. He is a writer, not a performer, and that was what was so wonderful about the way he read it. There was no ego, no sense of Mike being conscious of himself; he just totally concentrated on Martin's words. It's not often that you see something so selfless. No one could have read his words better.

It also helped us all to know that we were fulfilling her wishes, giving her this day. All the cousins and aunties and uncles who were still alive came over from Northern Ireland. Friends of Annie's from years ago, who I knew, and newer friends and colleagues who I'd never met, were all there. I felt slightly like a freak, as I know I was giving people who'd never met me a fright. Annie and I look very alike and we have similar mannerisms. People kept saying, 'You're so like her,' and I became an obvious point of contact. It felt like my job was to be there if people wanted to say something about Annie, or if they wanted to be introduced to my mum, who was ensconced in the corner on the comfy chairs with the Northern Irish. It wasn't a day for me to grieve: I was on duty. It was a sea of faces, and every now and again a surprising but familiar face would appear.

My mum's best friend Marie, who has dodgy ankles, came all the way from Leicester, by train, on her dodgy ankles. How wonderful it was to see her there – so many childhood memories surfaced when I looked at Marie's still beautiful face. She and her husband had been friends with my parents in Northern Ireland, and they came back into our lives in the seventies when they rediscovered each other in England. We had never seen such a good-looking couple outside films, and their four daughters were all beautiful, too, but they were also funny and down to earth so we fell in love with them all immediately.

They came to visit us in Norfolk one summer. They had Spanish suntans and bikinis; we had pasty white skin and regulation school swimsuits. We became obsessed with them. Annie had been mortified by her black school swimsuit and was determined to be as glamorous as Marie's girls. She got a new one for when they next came to visit. In my mind she was about fourteen, but looking at the photos again recently, I can see that she's a skinny eleven year old, squinting into the sun and looking delighted with her new swimsuit. There had been a lot of trying on in the shop, as many were considered too grown-up even though they were the same kind as Marie's girls had. 'Too grown-up' meant something to do with something rude that we didn't quite understand. Too sexual is what it meant. Annie's new swimsuit was definitely not sexy; it was a sort of mushy pea green and looked like it was made of crimplene, but Annie loved it. Marie's girls had so many, they had spares. One day, we played a game that involved putting one of the spare bikinis on their dog. I saw my chance. I took the bikini off the dog and tried it on. It fitted me perfectly (I was about six years old and the dog was a mid-sized mongrel). My triumph was short-lived, however; the adults said that it wasn't hygienic to wear a dog's bikini. From then on Annie used that incident as a reference for our childhood: 'Mummy was so strict you had to steal your first bikini from a dog.'

Back in the pub in Kensal Rise, people were constantly introducing themselves to me. I met one of Annie's old class-mates, Siobhan Hayes, and an ex-boyfriend of Annie's (who I knew all about but had never met before) had travelled from Switzerland. We had an intense and wonderful conversation. It's strange to think that I'll undoubtedly never see him, or the scores of other people who were there, again, but I will always remember everyone who came that day.

I was strangely upset by an alarmingly dressed woman who told me that she could see Annie's aura and feel her electricity in the room – for some reason it made me want to punch her in the head. I didn't want anyone telling me what to think about where Annie was. I hadn't thought about where Annie was yet; I wasn't ready for that.

People obviously mean well; they think saying things like that will be comforting to hear, but it just seemed such banal rubbish. It belittled the awfulness of Annie not being alive any more. Any talk of her 'looking down on me' just made me angry. I know, I am not easy to comfort.

The function room at the pub was packed with people laughing and telling stories, some crying. I'll say it again, Annie would've loved it. Her funeral really was a help; it was so full of Annie, it was a memory I could hug close, like a blanket, a comfort blanket – which I believe is also how people describe the feeling of taking heroin. A reassuring numbness before I had to start grappling with the reality of grief. I had no idea what was coming.

20

New Situations

A couple of days after Annie died Martin asked me to come round to the flat. He wanted to get rid of her clothes and told me to take anything I wanted. He left me alone. I was aware that this was a significant moment, that I should *feel* this moment, but I still didn't know what it was like to be without her. I felt like I was in a film, like I was acting and doing the things that I had seen people do in films when someone dies. I put my face in a folded bundle of T-shirts and smelled them. I lifted my head out of the pile and waited for a reaction. I just felt a bit silly. Everything felt like a cliché. I laughed and told her I knew I was being a dick.

In the end I just took the little blue-and-white striped cap that she'd worn in the hospital. It's hanging in my bedroom and I see it every day. I think now that I made a good choice. It's private and personal, just a little thing, and it's not something I have to explain to visitors. It's something that captures so much.

If I had wanted to hear her voice, I could have phoned her mobile. She was often a guest on *From Our Own Correspondent* on Radio 4, so I could have found one of her episodes on iPlayer. It was something I thought about. Would it be nice to hear her voice? One last time? But it seemed pointless. Do people delete people from their phones? I couldn't. She's still there. It makes no sense but it just seems utterly heartless to delete her. If I live into my nineties, I'll just have a phone full of dead people.

What I wasn't ready for was scattering her ashes. Martin knew exactly where they were to be scattered – Annie had left instructions (of course she had). I just instinctively said, 'No, not yet.' I just couldn't contemplate doing something so final. You scatter someone's ashes when they're dead and I still wasn't completely convinced that she was dead. Over and over again, it was like a mental double take: Annie died? Yes, she died.

This feeling of loss is one of the stranger things that I have in common with my husband. Around five years earlier, his older brother had died suddenly of an aneurysm, aged fifty-five, leaving three children without their dad. What does that mean? It felt as if it should mean something; we had both lost our older siblings. Then his brother's wife, my lovely sister-in-law, lost her sister. She died of cancer exactly one month after Annie; she was the same age, fifty-seven. Then some comics died, people from my era of comedy – Sean Hughes and Ian Cognito.

'What the fuck is going on?' I thought. 'People around me are dropping like flies.'

And then came the slow realisation, a thought bubbling in my brain: 'You're at that stage in your life now, Jo.' Of course I am, I'm in my fifties. The menopause seems like a timely and trivial distraction. 'Get them all talking about hot flushes and night sweats and they won't notice that it's death they should be worried about.'

I'm a comedian. I make strangers laugh. I don't tell strangers about my problems. I am the first person to shout 'give it a rest' at those embracing this modern, selfie-fuelled world of

over-sharing, but after Annie died I couldn't stop the conversation in my head. I started writing about it, to try to get the
thoughts expressed and out of my brain. I'm acutely aware I am
not unique; I don't have a monopoly on grief. In the league
table of deaths I don't think a sibling gets highest ranking, certainly not above a child or losing your parents when you're
young or the love of your life. But it's still in the top four; it has
a place in the Champions League.

Fifty-seven years is a lot more than many people get, but
it's also a lot less. My mother is in her nineties now and still
in good health, so you kind of presume you'll get the same
lifespan. People live longer now, don't they? Statistically, yes,
but not everyone. Annie's best friend Sarah said to me, 'You're
changed for ever now.' I didn't get it then. I do now, and of
course she was right. I am.

For the first couple of months after she died it was like a
punch in the stomach, forty or fifty times a day. I felt so stupid
for not knowing she was going to die. Not just in the hospital
and the hospice but throughout our lives. That I had gone
about my business not knowing that my sister would only have
fifty-seven years, like a film where I didn't see the ending coming. Where you're totally invested in a character and then: 'No!
What? She just dies?' No. There must be more . . . It felt like
there should be someone I could go to. 'Excuse me, but Annie
Caulfield died – that's a mistake, isn't it?'

At first I found it hard to say out loud – it's awful to say –
'My sister died.' There were new situations that I hadn't learned
how to navigate. You don't know they're coming. I was doing a
charity lunch – a posh do in Knightsbridge (not my world, but it
was for charity) – and I was to be the after-lunch entertainment.

It was all women. Women who were so posh that they seemed like a different species. Tiny ladies of indeterminate age dressed in bright colours, green and orange and pink, clothes that were clearly expensive but that they might have been wearing since 1972.

The lady who was sitting next to me reminded me of Princess Margaret – a fun, permatanned knocking-back-the-wine type, but with something tragic and stoic about her. She said things that just threw up a whole world yet she said them so casually: 'I loved cocktail hour so much that I wasn't really interested in being a mother and putting the children to bed – terrible, isn't it?'

Her plastic surgery meant the bottom of her face didn't really move (or maybe that's just the way posh people hold their faces). Her son had served in Iraq; I mentioned that my brother James had done several tours in Iraq.

'Do you just have a brother?' she asked.

'No, I've got a sister as well . . .' Shit. 'I had a sister. She passed away recently . . . sorry . . . I've never said that before.' I couldn't see clearly for the tears swamping my eyes. An opera singer from the telly was on stage talking about the charity, and I was up next. Shit. The Princess Margaret woman grabbed my hand. She held it hard, almost fiercely, and said, 'That's awful. Truly awful.' The fact that her facelift meant she couldn't show much emotion was actually helpful; if I'd seen sympathy on her face, I'd have totally broken down and I had to get myself together. She told me quickly and matter-of-factly that she didn't have a sister but she had lost her best friend to cancer twenty years ago, and I knew immediately she understood. She knew. Sometimes all you need is someone else who knows what grief feels like.

She was the perfect person to be with to navigate answering that question for the first time. She doesn't know it but I will remember her for ever. Thank you, Princess Margaret lady.

Then I worried that the same situation would happen over and over again – how should I react? Was I going to be ambushed for the rest of my life? Did I need to be constantly on the alert for upsetting encounters?

What really helped with this was an old friend from school, Elaine O'Halloran, getting in touch. I hadn't seen her since we were fifteen. She messaged me through Facebook to say that she had lost her older sister Alison to cancer. I remembered Alison from school. She had died aged forty-seven. The message was just right. She apologised for reaching out if it was intrusive, but she thought it might be helpful. She then wrote some beautiful words about what a sister is and how you are connected, that it's like losing a part of yourself. She and her husband came to my show when I was touring near where they lived. We sat down afterwards and just talked and talked. One of the things we talked about was what you say or don't say in these situations when someone asks if you have any brothers or sisters.

It didn't actually happen again for ages, and when it did, it was someone I didn't know well and it was an indirect question so I just let it go by. I didn't mention that I even had a sister, let alone that she had died. It's not just that it takes its toll on you, saying it out loud; it's also the effect on the other person. They're just engaging in harmless small talk, so to suddenly lay a big drama on them seems unfair and a little selfish. They may have their own drama, you don't know.

I am quite good, however, at talking about it if it's to raise money for Macmillan or other cancer-related charities. It's a way of Annie still being in the world and doing something useful. She'd like that.

But at other times I feel it's just private and no one else's business.

I became very good at bawling my eyes out in public. Friends would say I was very stoic – they never saw me cry – but it was odd situations with strangers that filled me with sadness and made me feel totally alone.

I realise now that I don't have the emotional resilience you need to tour around the country totally on your own, but I didn't know that then; I thought I was the same person I was before Annie died. On one journey an announcement came over the Tannoy that the direct train to London had been cancelled. I immediately burst into tears. My big sister had died and now my train had been cancelled – it was all too much. I asked the guard which train I had to take for London. He explained it very clearly and patiently. He seemed to think I was crying because I had to change at Didcot Parkway. 'It's a very easy station to change at,' he said gently. He was so nice, and even helped carry my suitcase up the stairs, that it made me start crying again. Although, as it turned out, it wasn't that easy to change at Didcot Parkway.

I tried to prepare myself for situations that I thought were going to be very emotional, so that I'd be ready to deal with them, but that didn't work either. Annie's actor/director friend Dan was over from LA again and had got in touch. When I first moved to London I'd acted in some of my sister's plays with him. He emailed me to say that he was doing a play in London and we must meet up. I went with some old friends, we watched the play and it was all fine. Then Dan came up to me. I was so surprised by my reaction – I simply couldn't speak. I was like a toddler struggling to explain through tears. Not a single word came out of my mouth, just snot out of my nose. Dan said to take my time, to sit down, take a breath, but I just waved him away and left. I couldn't do it. I knew no matter how long I sat down I wouldn't get myself together. Maybe it was because I had known him so long ago, when all three of us were young and thought we'd be around for ever. It was just overwhelmingly sad.

My friends helped me to the Tube. I felt wobbly and strangely exhausted. One of them said, 'Well, that's one way to get out of the post-show "You were marvellous, darling" conversation.' That made me laugh so much – that happy-sad cry that makes your knees buckle underneath you. Annie would've liked that.

Then another old face from the past appeared when I was hosting an awards ceremony in Manchester. I wanted to tell Annie all about it . . .

You'll never guess what, Annie. Christine was there. Yes, Christine from the pub we worked in in Notting Hill . . . Christine who drank whisky and coke A LOT! THAT Christine!

What a laugh we had back then in that tiny kitchen making the food for the pub. And the owner who had a Porsche and was so clearly using the pub as some sort of money laundering front. She went out with that guy who worked for the photographer Lord Lichfield; they'd come in from his studio round the corner for their lunch. She played the sax, and was in the band in your play about the blues player Champion Jack Dupree.

It's a weird coincidence because Martin recently gave me a picture of you and Christine that he'd found – it was an old press cutting from The Stage *newspaper. You were twenty-five.*

She was so excited to see me at the awards, Annie, and she looked exactly the same as she did back then – the same cute pixie face.

'How's Annie?' she asked. 'Oh, she used to make me laugh so much!' She beamed with happiness at the memories.

And I had to tell her that you'd died. It was weird; I didn't want to ruin her night. It felt like I was reporting on someone else who'd died, not you. I said it quite calmly.

Do you think I should have told her? I'll probably never see her again.

She said she could still hear your cackling laugh and she talked about all the plays you'd written and how funny you were.

Did I do the right thing? She didn't really NEED to know, she could be out in the world still believing you were alive – her exciting writer friend from the past.

Now, I think that I was afraid of my grief. Frightened of what I would feel, frightened I would burst open and it would be too terrible to deal with.

Back in Edinburgh, we had a guy in painting the house so we didn't have any pictures up and I developed a fixation about putting up photos of her. Did I want to? Could I bear it if I did? At the time I actually couldn't look at photos of her. It was like looking into the sun; I could manage a few seconds and then I had to turn away. I had to steel myself to look at her face; it was too painful. Is that common? I don't know.

So my irrational thinking on the photos was that I must put some up because that's what people did: they put up photos of their dead relatives. But I don't actually have photos up of anyone; it's clearly not a thing with me. Looking around, I was surprised to realise that there was only one photo up in the whole house, a picture of me and my husband at the Space

Needle in Seattle, and we only have that because they force you to have your picture taken. We look like we always look in photos: my husband looks like he's going to punch the photographer and I look worried because one day he may actually punch a photographer.

My brain rattled on. If I did put up photos of Annie, would it be horrible for my husband to come downstairs every day and see a photo of my dead sister? Would that then make him think of his dead brother? And why would I put up photos when I couldn't even look at a photo of her even briefly? And then what if people asked who she was? Then I would have to tell them about Annie dying and that would be awkward and awful.

I honestly thought about this for days; it was ridiculous. In the end I realised that random gasmen probably wouldn't ask about her photo, but I also realised that a lot of my friends in Edinburgh don't know what my sister looks like, so they *would* ask, 'Is that Annie?' And they might ask when I wasn't ready . . . so, as yet, no photos are up, but I do look at her blue-and-white cap.

It's wise to be cautious, though; your brain is just protecting you. I would try to pick safe times to think about her and to write things down, but of course that's never when my grief wanted to appear. But if my husband loaded up some new songs on my iPod, then my grief would appear, summoned up by punk rock versions of classic pop songs by a band called Me First and the Gimme Gimmes.

'It's punk rock!' my husband said incredulously.

He had carefully picked unsentimental music and here I was, three minutes in, bawling my eyes out to a punk version of 'Nothing Compares 2 U' (that did it, that song will do it every time). I was crying from my gut, a sound I'd never heard before, strangely like a pterodactyl or some other kind of dinosaur.

I've learned to be careful about music; it just injects itself straight into your emotions like shot-gunning a bottle of red wine.

In the first couple of months it was just so weird to walk around with this huge raw feeling that no one knew was there as I carried on doing normal things. Dropping off my dry cleaning; telling a cold caller that I haven't suffered whiplash in an accident that wasn't my fault; talking to my neighbour about bin collections; ordering drinks at a bar.

'Two bottles of Peroni, please, and my sister died three months ago.'

Grief is repetitive. Over and over again you want to say how much you miss them. But each time you miss them, it is its own emotion.

21

A Prime Location
and a Statement Coat

James and I with Annie's ashes in Battersea Park.

As Annie's birthday in May drew closer, I was suddenly desperate to scatter her ashes. For some reason it seemed important to do it before, like I wanted her to be 'settled in' for her birthday. Or that she seemed uncared for if her ashes were still in an urn on her birthday.

We gathered at her and Martin's flat and then walked down to Battersea Park to the exact spot she had asked to be scattered. It's one of the best addresses in London, overlooking the River Thames and on parkland that can't be built on. The ashes weren't in an urn; they were actually in what looked more like one of those cardboard tubes that usually contain a nice bottle of malt. I had no idea how to scatter ashes, but luckily, as a priest, James was an old hand at it. There's a bit of a knack to these tubes of ashes and we were surprised by how forceful James was (apparently you've got to give it some welly). He pushed the box right down into the shrubs and then released the ashes. That way the ashes don't blow away; they are sort of shot down into the ground. So if anyone needs ashes scattered, it appears to be a skill I have now learned.

That powdery grey stuff was my sister. It made me shudder, and I tried not to dwell on it; it seemed mawkish and unnecessary to think about it too much. But having somewhere to visit is very important. I can see why people erected pyramids and mausoleums, or filled Viking boats with stuff – pile it high, you can't do enough for someone you love.

It was continuing Annie's narrative of how she wanted things to be after her death. Later we got her a bench with a dedicated brass plaque (that would *so* appeal to her ego). She would've liked to have thought of herself as being the sort of person who gets a bench in Battersea Park, someone of whom strangers would say, 'She must've lived an interesting life.'

I know she's dead and that we do these things for ourselves, really, but it's *something*. It feels good to do *something*. It's like stroking her hand in the hospital; you never know . . . so it's worth doing. All that love and affection needed somewhere to go. We needed a place to bring flowers, or sit with her friends and chat about her, somewhere to be with her.

At Christmas we did up her shrub with Christmassy stuff. Stuff that was completely non-biodegradable and that the park keepers then took way. We often talk about 'the park keepers'. We've never seen them, but it feels like we have a relationship. I picture them in smart uniforms like characters in a comedy sketch from the sixties. In a way, they look after Annie: they must know something is going on at that shrub; it's not an accident there's flowers there. I also had a look at the plaques on the other benches: who would her neighbours be? I made up stories about the park keepers and the people attached to the names on the other benches, just like Annie would. She picked a good spot: plenty of visitors, but behind a rail so dogs can't wee on her, and right in the middle of London as she chose to live, sitting quietly observing, judging, thinking and writing.

Would it be too annoying for her that I would like to be scattered there, too? Not the same shrub, but maybe a shrub or two along. It's a happy thought. We lived next door to each other in the early eighties. It was in one of those lovely squares around a garden near Westbourne Grove, tall white buildings that are now worth millions but back then were divided into bedsits. We shared a bathroom with the owner, an old Greek man. He kept his bedroom door open and would wave at you from his bed as you passed by. He'd be surrounded by newspapers, on the bed and all over the floor, and we never knew if he read the newspapers or if they doubled as cat litter for all the stray cats that lived in his room – the smell suggested the latter. One day I went up to pay my rent as usual and he offered to reduce my rent if I showed him my fanny. I remember Annie saying, 'Tell me exactly what happened.'

'Well, he asked me to sit on his knee, which I did – it seemed rude not to – then he started talking about Cleopatra, so I got off his knee as I thought it was weird, then he asked me to lift up my skirt and make an old man happy, and that if I did, then I wouldn't have to pay all the rent. Then I paid all the rent and left.' Obviously, looking back, it seems outrageous, but we thought it was hilarious at the time. He never tried anything on again and I kept paying the full rent. Thinking about it now, God knows what he got up to; for all we knew, he might have gone into our rooms when we were out and got out our pants and tried on our bras while masturbating furiously (although I wasn't sure how mobile he was, so it might have been okay). It was also a bit weird that we all shared a bathroom, especially as it had one of those Victorian glass-panelled doors that meant you could see if someone was sitting on the loo (he seemed to sit on the loo more than was normal).

It was a weird and interesting place to live. There was a stripper, Gina, who lived across the landing from us with her seven-year-old son, who we sometimes used to babysit. Gina made very good money doing whatever it was she did, so didn't stay in the bedsits for long. Then there was Scottish Maggie – it was the eighties, we called people things like that then, plus she was the only Scottish person I knew at the time (although I'm not sure that makes giving her that nickname any better).

Scottish Maggie was always having raging drunken rows with her boyfriend and chucking his clothes out the window. Annie was quite taken with Maggie; I thought she was alarming and too old to be so wild. She was twenty-eight. I was nineteen and thought that people were meant to be proper grown-ups by the time they were her age and should have cars and live in a whole house. They certainly shouldn't go raging around swearing about Thatcher and everything being fucked. 'It's fucked, Anne! We need a revolution against the patriarchal society – that cunt can get tae fuck!' I think the irony of the statement was lost on all of us. (Incidentally, I still didn't have a car or live in a whole house when I was twenty-eight.)

Maggie left her job and set up a café in a Portakabin for the builders working on a construction site in Notting Hill. I thought that was very impressive, and it planted the seed of the idea that being self-employed was a thing, an inkling that it might be what I wanted. Maggie later got drunk and set fire to the Portakabin – I think there was something about her owing money, because a man came looking for her and then we never saw Scottish Maggie again.

Annie was still Anne back then. She had never liked her name (probably because she hadn't chosen it herself). At boarding school everyone called her Tom (her old school friends still do); at university she became Anne again; then at some point in (I think) the mid-nineties, she started referring to herself as Annie: 'Written by Annie Caulfield'. I've no idea what the genesis was. There wasn't a big announcement; it just gradually took hold and we all called her Annie. It suits her much more than Anne. Again it was her taking control of her life, renaming herself.

Scattering her ashes was mixed up with days when I was touring around, doing comedy shows. We scheduled it for when I was coming down from Scotland for work. It was a surreal jumble of normal life and grief.

'Are you just shopping and chilling today?' asked the young man in All Saints.

'Oh, do fuck off' is not an acceptable response, so I mumbled something along the lines of 'sort of' and didn't make eye contact as I moved away.

'Are you looking for something in particular?'

Christ, here he was again. As usual when I'm in All Saints, I wasn't quite sure what I was looking at. It takes me a while to work out which bit is the neck and which bits are the armholes, and whether the zips work or are just 'detail'.

I didn't even really know why I was there. I think I had a vague idea that I would need a warmer jacket because it would be cold in the park the next day. I must have been holding a coat because the super-friendly assistant said, 'That's a lovely statement coat. Are you looking for a statement coat?'

A statement coat? What a bizarre thing to be looking for. I almost laughed. Do you wear a statement coat with your statement hat? What if they're making contradictory statements?

Over-friendly customer service doesn't do what retailers think it does. It makes us leave your shop. I left.

'So what are your plans for the rest of the day? Up to anything nice?' asked the lady at the M&S checkout.

I wanted to say, 'None of your business,' but as usual reverted to something noncommittal and bland instead. I wanted to say, 'No, I'm not doing anything nice later. I'm going to scatter my sister's ashes. I'm frightened. I'm frightened of how it will make me feel.'

They always ask this at M&S Food Halls at train stations. I catch a lot of trains so I get it often, and it becomes increasingly annoying. Maybe we should embarrass them into stopping these interrogations?

'So what are your plans for the rest of the day?'

'Today? I'm having a smear test.'

Then go back to the same Food Hall a few days later. 'Excuse me, is Callum working? It's just I've got my smear test results and he was interested.'

I don't mind having a real, genuine conversation, but these are not real, genuine conversations. Some overpaid consultants thought it would be a good idea to force underpaid retail staff to talk to us; what they should do is pay their staff more so they'll be in a better mood and maybe start a conversation naturally.

It also seems never to have occurred to them that these questions might not always be appropriate, that a person (staff or customer) may not want to chat. That's why you shouldn't make your staff strike up inane conversations; you've taken away their natural human instincts. If a woman looks like she's been crying and doesn't make eye contact, maybe don't ask if she's having a good day.

Rather than make the world feel friendlier, you've made us all feel like customers. Customers that *have* to be spoken to.

'Have you come for something nice in the area?' asked the receptionist as I checked into a Premier Inn. It was an odd question as this particular Premier Inn was between a Tesco Extra and a service station, just off some outer, outer ring road. There was nothing nice in the area.

What I should have said is, 'Yes! I'm hoping to go round the petrol pumps later. Are they Roman? I've heard they're Roman.'

But then it was just the usual: 'Would you like to join our mailing list?'

'Um, no, not really.'

'We just need your email – then we can tell you all about our offers.'

'Um, no, thanks, if you don't mind.'

'We get some really great offers . . .'

Jesus! Please stop talking to me! I feel vulnerable. I didn't realise how bad I would feel. It's five and a half months since my sister died of cancer. She was fifty-seven. I suppose you can't know what it's like until someone you love dies before their time, but I do know that I want you to take your big, over-friendly, aggressively smiley head away from me.

At the Pret A Manger in King's Cross I had a moment with the young Spanish man serving me; we both rolled our eyes at the man beside me who was being rude and an arse to the other barista. He said I looked tired. Which was true, I did look tired, and it was just nice to have someone be genuine.

Maybe I have more of these interactions than most people because of my work, but some days it just feels like a relentless assault course of insincere, meaningless chat.

'You got a lot of plans for the weekend?'

'Just work . . .'

And thinking about my dead sister. I don't write that to be dramatic – that's honestly what came into my head. Annie would have laughed. She had a cackle that would burst out of her; it could simmer like a *Beavis and Butthead* snigger and then, bam! Full cackle.

Again and again. The same repetitive thoughts. How long before you can really grasp that someone is not here any more? Because of being sent to boarding school I saw Annie more than I saw my mum, so she was more than a sister to me. Maybe that's why this feels so awful. It seems a stupid thing to say, but I was shocked at how awful grief feels. I didn't know.

When the lady at Boots says, 'Sorry to have kept you waiting,' I feel bad. I can't have been waiting for more than three seconds. She's probably having a bad day, too. It's easier for her to say it to everyone than to really engage and notice if people have actually been waiting in a queue.

There's something very inhuman about this corporate 'human touch'. It's hard and brittle, more *Nineteen Eighty-Four*, *Westworld* or *Stepford Wives* than a friendly global village shop or whatever it is they think they're creating. The woman in Boots was about my age, and if she hadn't been ordered what to say, I might have ended up telling her what I was thinking. I was remembering my sister buying blue Rimmel eyeshadow in the seventies.

Shopping had become painful. I wished Talking Heads weren't on Tesco's playlist. I bought *More Songs About Buildings And Food* because Annie liked them. When she was about thirteen she wrote the band names Bad Company and Focus in biro on her plimsolls. She went off them quite quickly, but it was too late: she'd already ruined her plimsolls. She managed to turn Focus into a big biroed flower, like something from *Tattoo Fixers*, ahead of her time. And I remember when she had yellow hair with blue streaks. She wrote a musical set in a supermarket where the cast of characters included Catwoman, Picasso, Mae West, Louis Jourdain and Emma Peel. What a fabulous brain.

Oh, Annie, I really want to tell you about 'the statement coat'. It would make you laugh.

'How are you doing today?' asks the Costa man in Milton Keynes.

Not great today. Sometimes I'm okay, but not today. I scattered my sister's ashes yesterday. I know she liked where we put her ashes, but she would have liked it to be in thirty years' time.

22

Instant Coffee

I think it took me two years to realise that Annie had died. The first anniversary of her death was like her dying again; I thought of it as one year *until* she died, not *since* she had died. It was the second anniversary that hit me like a dull blow. She wasn't on a writing trip. She wasn't coming back, yet . . . I still had her and always would.

It had seemed indulgent and sentimental to me when people talked about what age someone would have been if they hadn't died. In the past I had scoffed when people shared such posts on Facebook, but in the two weeks leading up to her birthday I couldn't stop thinking about her – how fucking unfair it was, how mad she would be if she knew she didn't make it to fifty-eight. Birthdays and anniversaries are important to me in grieving: I can't help it, they are just a 'thing' with me. I didn't think they would be, as I'm not remotely bothered about celebrating birthdays in life, but they are.

In our little group I seem to be the one who organises and pushes to meet up. Spending time with people who knew and really got the complicated person Annie was has been a huge comfort. Nothing else can bring you closer to the person you loved; it's almost like spending time with them again.

Some people may like to 'move on'. I worried if I was wallowing, if I was hurting myself by swimming in these thoughts of Annie, but it's a sweet sadness to think about her. I don't go around talking about her with anyone except this little gang of Annie's.

On her birthday I thought again about how she used to get up at six in the morning to write, and about how I went to see her first play in London when I was still at school and she was at university in North London. The play was performed at Jacksons Lane community theatre, opposite Highgate Tube station. It was called *Opsed* after those open and closed signs that you used to get at garages years ago and which sometimes got stuck between open and closed so said 'Opsed'. One of the main characters said that was how he felt, neither open nor closed. I, of course, thought it was the cleverest thing I had ever heard. Near where we lived in Rutland there actually was an old sign like that and I took Annie to see it. I still have the photo of her standing next to the 'Opsed' sign.

★

Annie introduced me to her friends after the play. She always did that, as though I was a grown-up and there wasn't nearly a five-year age gap between us. It was terrifying. My main memory of that night was that I was on my period and had run out of tampons. Where did you get tampons in London? I whispered my predicament to Annie. Apparently in London you just strolled over to some random women in a bar and asked if anyone had a tampon. They did and they gave them to me. 'Should I give her money?' I asked. 'No,' said Annie, 'it's not lucky heather.' There were so many things about that I didn't understand.

I thought about her first school trip abroad – what an effect that had had on her. She was fifteen, and she was going on a very holy trip for good Catholic girls. To Rome: the seat of Catholicism, the home of the Holy Father. Annie loved it, not because of the Pope but because it was like nothing she had ever seen. This was how to live. 'The men look like film stars and everyone lives in apartments, in beautiful old buildings all on top of each other. Everyone's out on the streets at night, and they sit around talking and drinking coffee in cafés. No one lives in boxy houses.'

She was disgusted with our boxy house. I had looked around at our fifties red-brick Air Force house. I thought it was quite a nice house, but apparently I was very much mistaken. 'It's a godawful house in the middle of a field.' We were living in Nottinghamshire at this point, and like all Air Force bases, our base was, kind of, in the middle of a field. There were no cafés for miles around and people drank instant coffee that they'd made themselves in their own houses – what sad, tragic people we all were. I was upset that she was so angry about our house and our terrible life. But I was on her side. I thought, as always, that she was right, even though it was going to be difficult to get my parents to move to Rome.

But luckily, till that happened, there was an hourly bus to Nottingham that stopped on the A46, five minutes from our house. That bus took you to the Golden Egg on Maid Marian Way, where you could drink coffee made from an Italian machine and pretend that life was exciting, pretend that you were in Rome.

The other thing I thought about was something she said at the very beginning of her cancer treatment: 'It could be worse. What if I'd had a child?'

Annie and Martin had moved to Ramsgate for a short time. An experiment, they didn't stay long. It was a painful but hopeful time. They had tried to get pregnant through egg donation. Annie was in her forties when she met Martin. He was the love of her life, but was it too late for a family? After several attempts she did get pregnant, but the baby died in the womb; she was told that the heart just stopped. That was it: the baby was gone. The anguish and pain of that whole process was enormous, but Annie and Martin came through it, their relationship stronger than ever. I didn't know everything that went on then but I remember being excited, too. I thought I would be an auntie and had little daydreams about what Auntie Jo would get up to with her niece or nephew. I had so hoped it would work.

Annie had written a play called *Credit Card Baby* for Radio 4. It was the most personal work she had ever done, brave and honest.

This is the preview article she wrote for *Standard Issue* magazine (in both the play and the article she changed Martin's name to Sean).

One Little Dot

I have a play on Radio 4 this month, and some people won't like it. They might hate the writing, fair enough. But I know the content will bother quite a few people, because it reflects a largely positive view of egg donation.

The play was tough to write. I usually say what I think by dramatising other people's lives, from Dusty Springfield to soldiers in Iraq, but in this play I risked a version of myself and my partner: let's call him Sean.

The story happened because I fell in love too late. I was 40 and Sean – this funny, good-looking, soulmate of a 40-year-old man – turned up at a party. He ended what had been an interesting single life. You know the kind; where you seem really adventurous and independent, but you're too lonely, too often.

A year later, we were still happy. We started noticing friends over 40 pairing off and having babies. Why didn't we try?

We tried: we did tests. His sperm were jumping but my eggs were really not worth the bother. Even using them for IVF I'd have a 5% chance. But I'd have a 40–60% chance with donated eggs. This meant going private to use the satellite service my London hospital ran with a clinic in Valencia. We would pay a Spanish donor and clinic expenses; we would be travelling to Valencia quite a few times, paying flights and hotel bills . . . But a child mattered so much more than money.

Why go abroad? A change in British law in 2005 ended anonymity for donors. British donors became few and far between. The traceability makes both donors and recipients nervous.

For the donor, the procedure is intrusive, needing general anaesthetic, and there's a risk of ovarian hyperstimulation – a condition that sometimes results in life-threatening illness. British donors are paid a few hundred pounds. The £1,000 our Spanish donor was paid to cover expenses, time and risk seemed fairer.

Our donor was a woman in her late 20s who'd already had her own children. She received regular health checks and was as close a match to us as could be found across the continent.

While she had injections to stimulate egg growth, I took hormones to get my womb ready. The hormones made me nuts and it seemed the call to rush over to Valencia would never come. But it did. The donor's eggs had been harvested with a fine needle while she was under anaesthetic and successfully fertilised with Sean's sperm.

In the state-of-the-art clinic, I was comfortably fully conscious and hooked into stirrups while a glamorous female gynaecologist implanted two embryos through a thin glass tube. Sean watched the monitor with me. Tiny dots on a screen. Two for better chances, although twins are common in donor pregnancies.

There were four more fertilised embryos frozen as back-up. We needed them. In London a pregnancy test told us the implanted embryos had not taken. This was miserable but I started the hormone process again and we went back to wait in the hotel in Valencia.

The morning of the procedure the gynaecologist called. The embryos hadn't survived the unfreezing process. This was rare but it happened. If we'd like to try again, at a reduced fee ... I was so angry and wretched I refused. Sean said: 'Let's take a walk and talk about it.'

We walked. I realised I couldn't give up yet either.

This time it worked. One little dot was thriving. A sonogram in the London clinic showed me a tiny heartbeat. I was really pregnant.

Health and safety rules meant Sean wasn't allowed in the sonogram room. All he had was a printout of the scan but the nurse in charge was a sweetheart, I was sure she'd bend the rules. I was going to ask her when I went in for a scan on the edge of the three-month mark.

But the heartbeat had stopped. Just quietly like that, our baby had gone. I met Sean outside the hospital and howled in the street like a wounded animal. I couldn't bear it. Neither of us could bear it for a very long time.

My physical exhaustion and the misery we were sunk into meant that trying again would be too horrible. We discussed adoption for a while but it just didn't feel right after we'd come to love the little heartbeat so much.

We clung together, getting stronger, closer because of this. Except I secretly couldn't leave it alone. I started looking at internet sites telling me what I'd done was abominable; that disreputable clinics bought eggs for next to nothing from very poor women putting their health at great risk; that I was involved in a form of human trafficking; that donor children would feel a terrible lack from not knowing their origins ... On and on.

The negativity was aimed at women who'd left it too late. But women could be avoiding passing on inheritable diseases, or have suffered very premature menopause. There were many other reasons.

I found groups holding public debates about the scientific and sociological implications of egg donation. There was so much I hadn't thought about. Should the child be told? Should this be regarded as something as distant as organ donation? As casually as sperm donation?

One debate, held at university, had a heckler shouting about the sanctity of life. A panellist came back at him: the first egg donor baby had been born in 1983. We needed to accept that decades of science fiction nightmare hysteria were holding back proper discussion and a proper environment for children not born through traditional biology to grow up in, so they didn't feel freakish. The panellist concluded ferociously,

'And don't talk to me about the sanctity of life on this planet, when half its children are dying of starvation, thirst, preventable disease. Right here they're injured and psychologically scarred with atrocious cruelty from biological parents, or social alienation ... Children that are fed, thoughtfully loved and kept sane, wherever they come from, that's what the world needs. Not arguments about how they got here.'

Enough listening, I thought. Time to take a deep breath and write my story.

I've a thousand words here and the play is only 45 minutes. I wish there was more said that accepted how many successful donor children there are in the world now. It's time to have calm conversations, thoughtful strategies and widely accessible information for donors, recipients and, most importantly, for their children.

Credit Card Baby, starring Helen Baxendale and Ciarán McMenamin, was broadcast on BBC Radio 4 on 30 April 2015.

Ramsgate was where they would've lived if they'd had a child; it wasn't a place they wanted to live without being a family. I don't think she meant what she said in the hospital. She would still have loved to have had a child. I think she was being dramatic in her Annie way but also casting around for 'a reason'.

23

Question Everything

With Mum in Darley Dales, Derbyshire.
We were visiting Annie on her first year at boarding
school. I was wearing a white nylon lace blouse –
didn't care how scratchy it was, I loved it.

When my mum talks about Annie it's about Annie as a child. The Annie she talks about is a very different person, the confident, chatty toddler who would escape from the garden and just wander off to chat to people in the town when she was only three years old. What happened to that little girl? Was it just that after exposure to school and life, the chatty toddler wasn't so chatty or self-assured any more?

My cousin Francis said Annie was 'troubled'. She said it questioningly to see if I was okay with that description, and she said it with love and understanding. Annie *had* been troubled,

and I loved Francis for saying it, for including it in the complicated, funny, clever ball of things that my sister was. It was said
matter-of-factly. Sometimes all you want when you're grieving
is for people to really have known the person and to say something like that – something that tells you they 'got' her.

After Annie told me she'd been diagnosed with cancer
I remember it was when I told my husband that it hit me. I
started crying and said, 'It's not fair, it's so not fair. She hasn't
been dealt an easy hand.'

Annie got the addiction gene (there's a lot of it on both
sides of the family), although when I said I was lucky I didn't
get it, my husband pointed out that it took me ten years to stop
smoking. And who knows if cancer is lurking in me somewhere, biding its time?

By her mid-twenties Annie had realised she was a bad
drinker. Friends who knew her when she was drinking say that
she was a fun drunk, brilliant fun. At one party when I was
about eighteen or nineteen she turned on me, snarling, spitting
half-truths that really hurt because they were . . . half true. She
did it to a mutual friend on another occasion. I think he was
the one who first told her that she shouldn't drink. This pattern
repeated itself for a few years, the not being able to have just a
few drinks, the getting out of control, the turning nasty and,
when she went too far, the friends telling her to stop drinking.

There wasn't a dramatic announcement. She didn't want
to be a mean drunk, so in her mid- to late twenties she just
stopped drinking alcohol socially. She didn't talk about it, she
didn't say, 'I don't drink' (she didn't want to be treated like a
freak) – she just wanted a mineral water and lime.

After that she only ever hurt herself with alcohol. She could go for months without drinking, but maybe three or four times a year she would binge drink. It wasn't fun. She would drink at home on her own for days at a time. She didn't like the taste of alcohol so she would drink vodka and orange or vodka and pineapple.

She would call me, but only, I realised later, when she had done most of her drinking. She would call when she wanted to stop, but not before that, because she *wanted* to drink. Sometimes she would think I wouldn't notice. Once we went to the cinema and she kept nipping to the ladies with her half-bottle. As soon as I called her on it, then that would be her cue to sober up. One time she answered the phone, we talked for about half an hour and I said I would come round. When I got there she couldn't understand how I knew she was drinking. It was quite simple; she would have late night conversations in the middle of the afternoon. On this particular occasion she told me she was going to emigrate to China. She'd called the Chinese Embassy and they were going to give her a house and a year's worth of rice because she was an artist. She'd called several friends and told them she was emigrating to China. She was aware of the performance; there was always something dramatic but comedic in the tragedy of it. She then kept saying, 'But what about the Chinese? They're expecting me.' Smiling at me like a naughty child who knows they're being both bad and amusing.

Another time she went full Bette Davis – there were empty vodka bottles lined up by the sink. It was heartbreaking to see what she had done to herself, but it was also funny; ever the writer, she had set the scene. We both laughed when I pointed it out to her. The whole 'arrangement' was so dramatic – 'Look what I've done!'

In one of my favourite books of hers she writes about alcohol. *The Winners' Enclosure* is loosely based around her visit to Australia to trace the story of our long-lost Uncle Caulfield (did he become the Caulfield of the Caulfield Cup at Melbourne Races?). She didn't get on with Australia. She spent a miserable three months there, but on the upside, that was when she could be at her most hilarious and articulate. She loathed the macho, back-slapping, outdoorsy drinking culture and the racism. The book is scathing, heartbreaking and powerful. She was deeply affected by the devastation that alcohol had wreaked on the First Nations people and the lack of sympathy or help from the state.

I remember reading this passage from the book over and over again.

It seemed to me that all half the white population of Australia wanted to do was drink as well. From the wine toppers of middle-class Melbourne to the shouting vomiters of Cairns – it was something they could shake off with a line of cocaine before work, or a day's energetic water activity. For the Aboriginals it was the kiss of death to their otherwise chronically diseased lives among the whites. Among but not connected, not even registered.

I've been a chronic alcoholic. It's not something you want to be. I had friends who fought me to haul me out of it; I could pay for therapy; I had prospects I was throwing away for it. I got in, I got out. The thing I know about alcoholism is that no one knows much about it. Why some people can't drink, why entire races can't drink. It's genetic, it's chemical imbalance, it's inherited behaviour; it's a response to abuse – it's some and all of the above. And something else besides, in the ferocity with which it can possess you.

I've a friend who worked in a drug and alcohol centre for Native Americans – she told me the thing I most understood when everyone was trying to make me stop.

The Native Americans who don't drink or take drugs are very un-judgmental of the friends and relatives they have to keep bringing back to the rehab centre. They say these people have a hole inside them. They're hollow so they're more brittle, they only feel strong if they can fill themselves and in a lot of their circumstances there's only one guaranteed fill. Love, achievement, self-worth, a sense of purpose – they're a complex ballast to find and balance so that you're weighted right inside – and you can't buy them.

Western psychologists will tell you much the same. It's like a hairline fracture in your psyche. You may never get another blow to it to make the break happen. Sometimes it takes several blows, but once your soul breaks open like that, the space gapes open. Always. You can stop drinking but you're never safe till the space is filled. Anything else is just a holding pattern.

Anthropologists have discovered, among many remarkable things about them, that the Aboriginal Australians hadn't developed any process of fermentation. Worldwide most peoples produce an alcoholic drink, even if its use is restricted to and purely ritualistic. But the Aboriginals never had. So when a majority of a continent's race has been systematically murdered, displaced, exploited, ridiculed, impoverished, vilified and at the same time provided with a substance that seems to ease the wretched emptiness of such a tearing out of their hearts – it seems to me the final and cruellest act of spite, to despise their alcoholism and drug addiction.

I would hope that even if I hadn't been to the lowest, darkest part of drinking, that I'd still have felt so upset to see all the passed or passing out alcoholics in Cairns. But for the first time in my recent life I was glad about me and alcohol because it added fear to what I felt at every desperate drunk I passed. I'd feel the same pang of fear when I saw a drunk lying in a doorway in London. Frightened for them, frightened for me. I'd been a sliver of glass away from it. People don't do this to themselves because they want to. They can't come out of it when there's nowhere else anyone wants them to go.

I love that book. She wasn't someone who revealed herself often, so the power and accuracy of her exposure hits hard.

We would talk about why she drank and the feeling it gave her. There seemed to be no particular trigger. Sometimes things would be going well, she wouldn't be down and it was more if the opportunity was there. If she had some free days, she couldn't resist curling up and letting alcohol make her better. To fill up that hole, to numb her. At the same time as it was a comfort, she also knew she was punishing herself. But for what? Always this feeling deep down that she deserved to be punished.

When Annie was drinking she would be very ill afterwards. She didn't eat when she was drinking, she just drank and smoked. I can't help but wonder whether this is when the damage was done; in these years, did that lead to her lung cancer? We, her family, should have looked after her better, not let her do that to herself. We should have loved her more.

She worked so hard to close 'the space'. Why was that feeling so much worse in her than in me? Was it because I had her, an older sister who looked out for me? And she didn't. She had to make her own way. I could follow behind, learning from her experiences. What had made that chatty little girl feel so bad about herself?

As she got older the binging got less and less and then she didn't phone me any more. She phoned Sarah. Selfishly and stupidly, I was hurt that she didn't phone me: it was *our* thing. But, quite sensibly, she didn't turn to me. She had realised that I wasn't helping her stop. And she really wanted to stop so she had to go to someone who wouldn't let her get away with it.

Sarah dragged her to an AA meeting. Annie hated being at the AA meeting so much that she swore to Sarah she'd never drink again if it meant she didn't have to go to another meeting. She did not want to be defined in any way by alcohol and thought AA was set up to do just that. She didn't believe half the people were even alcoholics: 'They're just a maudlin bunch of losers boring everyone to death with their tedious stories.' But to be fair to AA, Annie never drank again, so it sort of worked.

She worked on herself a lot in her thirties, but quietly; she found a therapist she respected, someone who wasn't, as she put it, 'an annoying moron'. I think, rightly, that she saw therapy as a tool to help you in life, to help you fulfil your potential, and not something that should *be* your life. Above all, it should never be used as conversation. To Annie, therapy was to be done with a professional in a professional setting, and boring people with it was like describing your bowel movements at a party.

She'd mentioned writing about the way we deal with addiction and what it is in your brain. Looking up figures randomly online, it says the success rate of AA is only between five and ten per cent. The success rate of outpatient therapy is thirty-five per cent and residential long-term treatment is sixty-five per cent. Clearly, I'm dabbling in an area where serious people do serious studies, but there's a discussion to be had, and this might be useful to someone. And Annie valued being useful very much. We, the state, are not giving people anywhere near enough help to break free of their addictions.

It was so Annie to question AA. It was like the nuns all over again: question everything. To her, AA was consigning herself to never being free of the influence of alcohol, and that wasn't good enough. She wanted to kick it in the head and leave it for dead. I see it where I live in Leith in Scotland; all the local chemists do a roaring trade in NHS methadone. It contains 'the problem', but 'the problem' is people, people who are condemned to a half-life, to just existing and never knowing what they could've been without drugs.

One of my favourite plays of hers, *Didn't Die*, is set in a women's prison. I think there's a lot of 'troubled Annie' in it – the humour, the vulnerability and the 'badness'. She did workshops with female inmates at Holloway Prison. The 'badness' is not criminal: it's the fighting back against unfairness, it's arguing in 'polite conversation' because you can't let people get away with talking shite, it's wanting to upset the establishment, it's wanting to push people away. Also, as Annie found out and identified with when she worked with these women, the badness is being bad to yourself. The self-harm comes in so many forms.

When Annie died I drank more. I drank pretty much every day for two years. Which sounds ridiculously melodramatic. I wasn't drinking a lot, just a large glass of red wine to fill that hole and knock me out, but I was drinking daily. I often drank on my own in hotel rooms (I was away working – I didn't specifically book a hotel room to drink). I had never done that before, though, drinking alone; it felt strangely glamorous and tragic. I was aware of Annie and that I didn't have the fear; I had the comfort of knowing I would stop. If I was in primary school, I think they would say I was 'acting out'. I totally understand why kids do that now: something horrible has happened, something that hurts you and you want to stamp your feet and be bad just to show how hurt you are. It was such a tame way to be bad. I would buy a small bottle of red at M&S or at the hotel bar, and sometimes I would buy a glass at the bar *as well* as my little M&S bottle. I know – pretty lame. Sometimes I just wanted to feel sorry for myself and wallow in the pain for a while, but with the pain numbed by alcohol. Normally I'm a very social drinker, but the attraction of this was doing it on my own. Preferring wine and my thoughts to the company of others. Although I wasn't alone, I was with Annie; I was spending time with my sister. With hindsight, I think it was okay to cut myself some slack. It wasn't the worst thing in the world to be doing.

Maybe a year after Annie stopped the binge drinking she met and fell in love with Martin. Like some terrible Hallmark card – *when she finally loved herself then she was able to love.* She and Martin were perfect together. When they first met he said to a friend of hers, 'I really like the way her brain works.' He got her. In the hospice he overheard her saying to a friend, 'Martin is such a perfect boyfriend. He couldn't be more perfect if I'd made him myself.' It made him laugh because it was a perfect example of her peculiar egotism. 'She's somehow managed to give herself the credit.'

I admired Annie enormously for beating that demon, for not letting alcohol define her.

24

Whitewashed Stairs and Cans of Red Stripe

Bridget Riley exhibition, National Galleries of Scotland, Edinburgh, 2019.

Eighteen months after Annie's death I was walking along Princes Street. It was a bright sunny day in August, and the Edinburgh Festival was in full swing. I'd just done a live podcast recording to plug my stand-up show, I was feeling happy and a little wired, and I decided to treat myself to twenty minutes rummaging through the racks at TK Maxx (TK Maxx only rewards those who take the time to rummage). Suddenly I was stopped dead in my tracks. It was as if someone had physically put their arm out to stop me walking. Straight ahead was a huge exhibition banner – *Bridget Riley* – and hanging down the side of the Scottish National Gallery were those familiar stripes and colours, soft dusty pink, blue and purple.

I wanted to say something, to just stop someone and say, 'Oh my God, Bridget Riley! I've slept in her house, I've drunk her booze when she was away and then had to replace it when she was due back . . . She wrote a beautiful handwritten letter to my mother when Annie died. She's part of my life, she's part of my sister.'

How strange to be connected to this world-famous artist by my sister. (I'm not saying me and Bridget are mates – our connection is that Annie had a job as Bridget's live-in cleaner/housekeeper in the eighties and they had kept in touch ever since.) All the memories came crashing over me. The times I climbed those four flights of whitewashed stairs to Annie's flat at the top of Bridget's house, the stairs and walls that Annie had kept pristinely white. When Annie got her own flat she had the floors painted like Bridget's. My mum has a cutting from *The Stage* about a play of Annie's; accompanying the piece is a photo of Annie at the corner of the road where Bridget's house is in West London. She's standing with sax-playing Christine who I met again at the awards do. The caption says: 'Writer Anne Caulfield, age 25.'

The details of where she was living before Bridget's are a muddle. We'd been sharing a flat off the North End Road, the unfashionable bit of Fulham at one point, but there were so many places that I can't quite remember, until she got the job at Bridget Riley's.

'A woman must have money and a room of her own if she is to write fiction' – turns out Virginia Woolf was right, although it doesn't necessarily need to be that much money. Having a flat included in the wages was a great thing for someone like Annie who wasn't good with money. She had the great combination of freedom, time *and* boundaries. Those stairs had to be kept white, the assistants in Bridget's studio had to be fed twice a day, and there were other odd jobs like laundry and shopping, but there were no set hours. The work just needed to be done, and when it was finished then Annie was free to write.

If you don't know of Bridget Riley, just google her. You'll recognise her work. She became well known in the sixties for her op art paintings and has been a seriously respected artist ever since. Op art makes her sound a little trivial somehow, and although her work inspired textile designers and the fashion world it is so much more than that. The viewer really does complete her work because she challenges the way your brain reacts when you look at her paintings.

Bridget Riley.

Annie admired Bridget and learned a lot about how to be an artist from her. How you have to structure your life around your work, and how hard you have to work. Being completely ignorant of art, it was a whole new thing to me that assistants would do a lot of the actual painting (filling in the stripes). The assistants were all artists themselves and all worked part-time. Bridget never wanted people to give all their time to her; they had to be able to pursue their own artistic work, too. I hate going into this in such a fleeting way, but it was wonderful that it was a female artist and that Annie saw that it's not about your gender: it's about the work you put in and being as selfish/ focused/dedicated as other, mostly male, artists are.

> I have never been aware of my femininity as such, when in the studio. Nor do I believe that male artists are aware of an exclusive masculinity while they are at work.
>
> – Bridget Riley, 'The Hermaphrodite' (1973)

As a woman, if you achieve any kind of success, you are constantly asked about your gender, and Annie, like me, always thought that it got in the way. I like this quote from Bridget in an interview for the *FT* by Richard Cork. It satisfies people by giving them a reason. Bridget was eighty-seven in this interview so had had a long time to come up with a good answer.

> I was extremely fortunate growing up during the second world war, from that point of view. Class structures disappeared under the demands of that time – we had to make a superhuman effort, all hands to the shell with Wrens, Land Girls and women working even in the most dangerous factories, too. Gender differences absolutely did not operate, and comradeship was very intense. After the war we all wanted to do something with the peace. It sharpens you.

It's a great answer, isn't it? But Annie grew up in the seventies, not during the Second World War, and I've a feeling that she and Bridget were just born like that. They didn't think their gender was something to sit around contemplating. Get on with your work.

Or, maybe, it was the example of our very capable mother, one year older than Bridget, who also grew up in wartime.

Martin put it more practically. He said, 'I don't know about Annie learning how to be an artist from Bridget. I think she learned that she'd really like to have someone do all the cooking and cleaning for her.'

An atelier, that's what her flat at Bridget's was. A perfect studio flat, like the ones you see in movies about struggling artists in Paris. It had windows that you could climb out of, and then sit on the roof and look out over West London. There was a small kitchen annexe where Annie always had a coffee pot sitting on the stove. She had simple and sophisticated tastes. I drank Thunderbird wine or Cinzano because they were cheap, and I always had instant coffee; Annie had good coffee and real butter and French bread. I tried to work out how she managed to make everywhere she lived look stylish and a bit French. Lilies in a jug – back in the eighties, that wasn't something you saw in every department store display like you do now. How did she know to do that? A black-and-white photo of someone artistic and interesting – a blues singer or a writer like Jean Genet – and good bedding, that's the secret. I think I've finally got it. Annie would never have anything in her home that she didn't like; she'd rather have had nothing. Where I'd buy the nicest cheap duvet cover from BHS (usually something in peach, hideous but affordable), Annie just had an old navy sleeping bag (dating back to our get-attacked-round-Europe holiday) unzipped on her bed, over a white sheet, and it somehow looked like an antique quilt.

I went to loads of parties in that flat; it was a crossover time in our lives. I acted in a play written by friends of hers, the set for which was designed by one of the artists in Bridget's studio. There were always after-show parties when Annie had had a play on. 'After-show parties' sounds very grand; it was basically a roomful of people with no money drinking cans of Red Stripe and cheap wine, but it was a *party* after *a show*. Parties full of actors, musicians, writers, cartoonists and people who did stuff or who wanted to do stuff – interesting people. This was the early to mid-eighties, and everyone seemed to be trying to be something. But it wasn't like people on *The X-Factor* trying to be famous; it was a different mindset. They just wanted to be involved. It was still very much the punk rock ethos that you could have a go, that it was okay to be self-taught. Youth is also what it was about, but you don't know that at the time – all this drive and energy, this willingness to take risks. Some of the people will peel off and go into a 'sensible job', but you don't know which ones they are yet.

Annie was at the heart of this. She had several plays on at the Old Red Lion in Islington, which was a hangout for actors from the Anna Scher Theatre and Central Drama School, and that's where she and Dan, who moved to LA, met. And there'd be people who were in *Grange Hill* and people who were starting to get work and who (like Kathy Burke) would later become very well-known. I remember staring at the actor Jerome Flynn, who was friends with a mutual friend. He had a job, a proper acting job, as did someone called Amanda Donohoe, who already looked like a star and had been Adam Ant's girlfriend, people said. She was far too glamorous and intimidating to be in a pub at The Angel. Acting wasn't as middle-class then as it is at the moment; people still got grants to go to drama school so you didn't need rich parents to subsidise you. There were people from all sorts of backgrounds in Annie's world. She used some of my rockabilly friends as the onstage band in one of her plays. My then-boyfriend Rocky was the inspiration for one of her early plays, *The Lighthouse Keeper*, which was about people who know who they are, people who live in their own slightly Bukowski-esque world.

Thinking back, she was great at getting all these different types of people to do stuff for her: design sets, make clothes, act, donate rehearsal space . . . She was living the 'big creative life' that she had wanted, the life she somehow knew about when she'd been a teenager in Norfolk. No one had any money, but Annie always seemed to have just enough to get by. You just needed money for fags, drinks and your bus fare home, our clothes were all from charity shops and no one owned any stuff. We didn't have mobile phone bills or cable bills or Spotify subscriptions. We got our records secondhand from the Record and Tape Exchange in Notting Hill Gate.

When she was offered a full-time job at the Riverside Studios in Hammersmith that's when she had to leave Bridget's. She'd become a paid writer with no more time for washing white stairs.

★

All this came back to me as I stared at the sign outside the gallery in Edinburgh. I wanted to go to Bridget's exhibition, to see those huge stripes that I had seen stretched out on the studio table being filled in, but I couldn't. I wanted to be able to savour it, to allow myself to feel, but mid-Edinburgh Festival is not the time for comedians to feel. I needed to keep my funny pants on.

Bridget had come to Annie's funeral. She seemed ageless, petite with messy short brown hair, still cool-looking. 'You must be Anne's sister, you look so like her,' she said. She held my hand. I don't remember what else she said, I was just so pleased that she had come and that she had valued Annie. It meant a great deal to my mum. Several times that day she said, 'Bridget came.'

I didn't go to Bridget's exhibition that day, I had to get home, get something to eat and then get ready for that night's show. I said to myself that I would go to the exhibition after the Festival – it was in Edinburgh until the beginning of October – but I didn't make it, and it bugged me that I hadn't gone. But part of me knew I had avoided it deliberately. I wasn't ready.

25

Denzel Washington and Sandwiches

What a photo! Annie working backstage in 1990
with Denzel Washington.

Annie always knew what she wanted to do. At her funeral, an
old school friend reminded me that she'd said she would be
a writer even then, at the convent. Such a funny mixture of
arrogance and insecurity. She never thought that she should
have a career path and get a proper job like teaching or whatever else adults did; proper jobs took up too much writing
time. Annie thought proper jobs were a weakness, something
to be resisted, that you mustn't be sucked in by the security and
comfort. Proper jobs were the death of creativity, and forgoing
the security that they offered was the sacrifice you made if you
wanted to make your living as a writer – and she did end up
making her living as a writer. It's hard to imagine Annie in a

corporate environment, especially if there was any 'blue sky thinking' talk. She'd be a great worker but wouldn't understand some things about being in a team. 'Why do we have to give a fiver and sign a card? I don't even like Karen in HR. She's a vile woman, and if she's leaving, she should buy *me* a card. I'm the one still working in this dump.'

That's not to say that she never had a job. She did loads of 'unproper' jobs for money: cleaning, bar work, supermarket checkouts, all hard work but never 'proper jobs'. I had the same idea about proper jobs and followed Annie's path, but without any clue about what I was meant to be doing. After boarding school, the only thing I knew for sure was that I never wanted to be told what to do ever again. I wanted to work for myself.

While at university and for about five years afterwards, Annie wrote and produced her own plays. She was always proactive (I remembered that when I eventually started doing stand-up: it's your work, so work at it). Annie was learning her craft. After a while, as a result of doing those shows, she got a good agent and a commission from a theatre company. Then, when she got the job as a script reader for Riverside Studios that's when things started to happen for her in TV. She met some producers and script editors looking for new writers. She met Lenny Henry and submitted jokes and sketches and they just clicked. In her late twenties she started getting her first jobs in TV, writing stand-up and sketches for comedy shows; she found comedy writing easy and did it off and on throughout her life.

I like this little piece that she wrote about working backstage and being the writer who thinks up the 'ad libs' for any star who needs a line on the day (and who also tells them where the sandwiches are).

Name Dropping for Charity

There are so many serious, analytical articles to write about big charity concerts. This isn't one of them. Although, having worked as a writer and script editor for the presenters on some of these concerts over the years, I do know one thing that isn't up for debate – surprise, surprise – everyone backstage is having a great time. Especially the non-famous likes of me, who run about clutching notebooks with our jaws permanently dropped.

Too young for Live Aid, my first big gig was at the 1990 Wembley concert to celebrate Nelson Mandela. He was free, and he was going to be there in person. Security alerts meant the running order kept changing, and I was one of the few to be kept in the loop. If they wanted to know where they were supposed to be, the presenters, including Denzel Washington, had to follow me around all afternoon. Oh, the things I've had to put up with for good causes . . .

Being shadowed by Denzel was, of course, overshadowed by the moment I got to shake hands with Mandela. Mandela was passing along a line of participants to thank us. Some managed to express their admiration succinctly: I made a sort of gurgling sound.

I've also shaken hands and gurgled at George Clooney – his fault for being even more handsome in real life. I've made a snurfling sound at Paul McCartney. I did manage something quite like a 'hello' to Susan Sarandon, and I discussed the demerits of instant coffee with Youssou N'Dour. I was even more debonair with Elton John, warning him to mind a step, and I told Kylie that the loos were on the left. James Brown, David Frost, Yo-Yo Ma, Bono, Annie Lennox . . . You name them, I've had inconsequential fragments of conversation with them.

Friends often tell me it's amazing that my writing life has led me to meet all these people. It would be better if I'd had witty things to say to them, or even elicited more than a look of alarm with my incomprehensible greeting sounds. Or not been so busy I couldn't manage more interesting banter than, 'Not yet, Denzel, have a sandwich.'

So in years to come, if chat shows are looking for a new Alan Bennett – a writer who has met everyone and can delight an audience with pithy anecdotes – maybe don't call me. But backstage for celebrity world-saving? I'm always up for that. Maybe after another twenty years, I'll learn to be cool about it.

Sometime in 1990, before I had any thoughts of doing stand–up, Annie took me with her to the recording of a TV show called *Paramount City* she was working on. It was a stand–up show filmed in a club environment. There was no lightbulb moment for me. I didn't watch that show and think, 'Yes! That's what I want to do!' There were some American comics on the show and they were the ones who really impressed me – I'd never seen anything like them. I have to confess that I don't remember any of the British comics on the show (don't be offended, I only saw one recording). I do remember that Denis Leary was on. I'd never heard of him, but he did a routine about a Barry Manilow keg party that blew my mind. It was the confidence of it, so cocky, his strutting around and smoking like a real movie star. A leather jacket, not a suit. The routines seemed so complex: how did he think of this stuff? It definitely felt like something that I couldn't do. Annie must have been one of very few women who were writing comedy then and, even more rare, a woman who was writing comedy for male comedians.

In the mid-nineties, I was addicted to the TV drama *This Life*. It felt like a new kind of television that showed how people actually were in real life – drinking and swearing and having one-night stands. Then Annie got a job writing on the second series – now it was the coolest show on TV!

But, typical Annie, writing for TV and getting well paid was all a little too comfortable and a little too much like a proper job. She had her own stories to tell, so she stopped chasing the TV work and started travelling more and writing books and radio plays. Writers are given much more freedom on the radio. There is so much money involved in television that executives are constantly poking their nose in and wanting things changed; shows in Britain rarely end up the way the writer wants them unless you're someone with a huge back catalogue like Russell T. Davies. Radio basically treats you like a grown-up: here are the words you can't say, this is the budget and it needs to be this many minutes long. The rest is up to you.

Annie covered some hugely different areas in her plays, from the war in Iraq to Paul Robeson and one of my favourites, the story of Gert and Daisy (real-life sisters Florence and Doris Waters), who were a hugely successful female comedy act in the thirties and forties.

I went to see one of Annie's plays being performed at Òran Mór in Glasgow shortly after she died. *Dusty Won't Play* was the true story of Dusty Springfield refusing to play in segregated South Africa unless black people were allowed into the theatres. Civil rights and injustice of all kinds had always been a theme in Annie's work. In 1993 she received a Race in the Media Award from the Commission for Racial Equality for her play *After You've Gone* about 1920s black entertainers Layton and Johnson. It starred Lenny Henry and Clarke Peters. Her play for Clean Break Theatre Company, *Didn't Die*, about women in secure prisons, won a *Time Out* magazine award.

I know she also volunteered at the Refugee Council. I'm ashamed to say I have no idea what she did there; it was just something that was part of her life, and she would mention it from time to time, usually a funny story, never her being 'worthy' or showing off about her 'good works'.

26

Greece by Bus and Sugar Spit

I didn't know it at the time but this was me leaving home.
Off to London to catch the Magic Bus to Athens, 1981.

Mother's Day was unexpectedly difficult. I felt a huge sadness pulling me down. It felt like Annie had died again, the bit of her that I hadn't realised I had lost, the bit of her that was like a mother to me. I hadn't fully grasped that having Annie was like having an extra mum. I don't know if that's a big sister thing or just her.

I felt that scraping feeling of loss, that screwing up inside my stomach, as I realised how much I missed her wisdom and advice, and that I would miss it for ever. A mum who's not your mum and who, like me, felt a bit odd and out of kilter sometimes. How reassuring it is to have someone in the world who is odd in the same way that you are. I remember phoning her from a hotel once when I was on tour – speaking to Annie always helped when I felt sad or lost or felt that I'd fucked up by having a weird life – and telling her that I'd burst into tears at a motorway services. I'd seen some sales reps getting in their cars and wondered if they ever had a little cry in the toilets when they were just on the road too much. Annie said she was sure that sales reps cried, too.

I often wonder what I would've been like without Annie. How much of me is me and how much of it is Annie? Or were we just born alike? Would I eventually have got into comedy if there had been no Annie leading the way? Would I have stayed in school and retaken my A-levels rather than running off to London at seventeen? I might've had a much more conventional life, or I might not.

After taking my A-levels I went on holiday to Greece with three school friends. We went on a Magic Bus (that sounds like we joined a cult – it was just a bus that set off from Russell Square and went all the way to Athens). This was before cheap flights, and it took two and a half days to get to Greece and you needed about five different currencies for all the countries you stopped in along the way (this was pre-euro and the Schengen Area, so you had to constantly show your passport – basically how things are now, post-Brexit). We stopped in what was then Yugoslavia, but none of us had any of whatever their currency was, so we just stared in café windows, salivating. Some old Greek ladies on the bus brought Primus stoves and heated up food they'd brought with them – they would've done well on one of my dad's beach trips. It was my first trip anywhere without Annie. We slept on beaches. That was a thing that was allowed then; well, nobody moved us on or complained. I remember my first night in Athens. We met some other young people and all got drunk in a restaurant. I thought I had never felt so happy. I was lying in the street singing and I looked up at my friends (they hadn't joined me) and all the tourists walking by and was completely unself-conscious and content. Just lying on my back singing 'Brass In Pocket'. Whenever I see young people drunk and out of control I remember the drunk seventeen-year-old me – what a great feeling it was.

Getting back to London on the Magic Bus obviously took the same amount of time as getting there, and I watched my tan flaking off as the bus made its way across Europe. Once I was back in London I went to stay at Annie's. I phoned home to get my A-level results (I think I got a B, an E and a U – they weren't good). My dad said I should go back, do another year at sixth form and resit the exams. Having a September birthday meant I'd always been a year younger than my classmates. I was still seventeen so could easily have done another year at school, but to me it seemed too humiliating to go back. I never even talked to my friends about it (friends who I later found out did go back and do their resits – in fact, one friend took four long years to finally pass his A-levels). I'd just had enough. I didn't want to live at home or go to school any more. Did Annie say that I should drop out and stay in London? I honestly can't remember.

It seems odd now that I never discussed any of this with my parents, but I think they were preoccupied with their own problems. Being with Annie in London seemed both safe and exciting. I felt at home being near her. I always did. She was the person who I would go to when I was in trouble; you didn't bother your parents. That might have been a hangover from the nuns. It was drummed into us over and over again that the biggest sin possible was to disappoint or be a bother to your parents. The biggest threat they could use was: 'Do you want your mammy and daddy to know about this?' There was always the subconscious fear that, if you disappointed your parents, they wouldn't come and collect you in the holidays, that they might just leave you at school with the nuns for ever. What an evil thought to put in a child's head, although, to be fair, it might only have been me that thought that. Part of me definitely felt that I had been sent away to school because I had done something wrong and that somehow my parents were happier without me.

Annie had told me how to get to her flat in Crouch End from King's Cross. When I got out at Highgate Tube I realised I'd lost my ticket.

'Did you come from Archway?' he said. (Archway's the stop before Highgate.)

'No, King's Cross,' I said politely.

'You mean Archway.' He laughed when I didn't understand he was trying to help me out. I think he even winked at me, but I still wasn't getting it.

'No, King's Cross,' I insisted.

'On you go,' he said and waved me through.

I apologise now to that ticket collector for being so ludicrously dense and unworldly. I then realised that my suitcase was far too heavy to carry and it was quite a walk from Highgate. I was dragging it a few steps at a time when a man in a white van stopped and asked if he could give me a lift. A complete stranger, in London, asked me to get in his van. Who would get in a stranger's van? Me. I would. And he turned out to be a nice man who just helped me by putting the suitcase into his van and dropping me at Annie's address. I was used to hitchhiking on my own in Rutland. I'd often hitch if I missed the school bus, so doing it in London seemed no different. The chances of being raped and murdered were equally high in both situations.

Annie, me, some waitressing friends, Adam and Daniel.
My shoes were from Red or Dead and I loved them.

Performing of some sort was what I wanted to do, but I was also shy and I knew nothing about anything to do with performing. I'd seen Victoria Wood and had a vague idea I'd like to be like her but wear nicer clothes. Annie's approval was important, and we were against being 'normal' or having a 'normal' job, but I was seventeen: was that Annie's influence or was that me? This was 1981. London was full of casual jobs where you could earn good money and just start living your life, so that's what I did. Annie encouraged me by giving me some acting roles in several of her pub theatre plays, and I got other parts in fringe theatre as well. I was good, but it didn't really lead to anything, or, more accurately, I didn't know how to make it lead to anything. Was it even supposed to lead to anything? Also I spent a lot of time being a rockabilly, learning to play the drums, being in a band and selling vintage clothing. That was nothing to do with Annie – that was all my own madness – but she approved. I was interesting. An interesting fuck-up.

When I eventually stopped being a waitress/rockabilly drummer/vintage clothes seller/barmaid and started to make my living as a comedian, I felt that it caused a difficulty in our relationship. She casually declared that she hated stand-up comedy, that 'it was puerile and stupid'. It almost made me laugh. You can't just say to someone, 'Yeah, that thing you do for a living that you love – I hate it!' But she did say that, and I let her. Maybe she did hate what I do.

Working my vintage clothes stall at a rock 'n' roll weekender,
Brean Sands holiday camp, near Weston-super-Mare.
Early 1980s – it's a blur.

Or maybe it's the age-old story of the older sibling resenting the younger one. When she was drunk she would say that she didn't know why she resented me and that she didn't want to resent me. The first time she said it, I thought, well, at least I know you do resent me. But it wasn't her fault. That was enough for me. I knew that she loved me and . . . relationships are complicated. Even now I can hear her voice saying that I'm making her out to be the bad one. I'm not. I'm just saying that our relationship changed, that we weren't in each other's lives so much for a while, that we weren't as close.

It came to a head one Christmas. I was meeting friends for dinner, and we were waiting for one last person. He arrived and said, 'So sorry, but I was at Annie's Christmas drinks.' I burst into tears. We'd grown so far apart that she would invite a friend of mine for drinks but not me. Now I can look at it logically and think, but I didn't invite her to the dinner I was having with my friends either, but I didn't see it like that then. My friend Gill gave me good advice. She told me to talk to Annie: simple but much-needed advice. I arranged to meet Annie for tea, and we met in Victoria station, as she said she didn't have much time. It all poured out. How I was so upset that we weren't close any more, and then she said that she thought I didn't want to be close any more. She said that I'd pushed her away and not included her in my life. She told me I hadn't been supportive enough when she was trying to get pregnant. I'd wanted to be supportive, but I didn't want to intrude. She had Martin. I didn't think she needed me; it was their private business, wasn't it? I had my own stuff going on at the time, so maybe I could have done more, could have shared more, but she could be a hard person to help sometimes. And so can I. I blubbed and blubbed and then she blubbed and we hugged. Honest to God, it was like an afternoon movie on Channel 5.

Who knows the rights and wrongs? Whatever they were, the situation had built up and built up to the point where it might have become insurmountable if we hadn't tackled it then.

She harrumphed, and then we started to be okay again.

We would meet for 'tea and nonsense' whenever I was working in London. Our favourite place was Maison Bertaux in Soho. We used to meet at Patisserie Valerie back when it was only one shop, but when we found out they'd become a chain and were opening everywhere – there was one in Hull, for God's sake – that was it. Like good Londoners, we never went back.

One day I got to Maison Bertaux first, which was unusual, as Annie was even more punctual than I am. It was a sunny but cool day, spring or autumn, and they'd opened the big doors and set up tables outside. I sat and watched as a homeless man went along the outside tables, spooning the sugar from the bowls into his mouth. It was like he couldn't believe there was free sugar just sitting there. He scooped it up with such glee that half of it fell out of his mouth back into the bowls. He smiled at me as he was doing it, as if to say, 'What a day, eh? Free sugar!'

I told Annie about it when she arrived. It was exactly the sort of thing that would make her laugh, funny and a bit odd but also joyful and life-affirming. Then she saw some people at the outside tables ordering coffee. 'We can't let them use the spit sugar,' she said.

Annie charged off to tell the French lady at the counter (we were both slightly in awe of her and thought she was very fabulous; we called her Madame Bertaux, but I doubt that was her name). The waiter came out and collected all the sugar bowls; he then said something to the French lady, who glared at me as only a fabulous French lady can. I said to Annie, 'Why are they staring at me?'

Apparently Annie had told them about the incident in French, 'but it all got a bit confusing so they may think that *you* spat in all the sugar bowls'.

Although she'd spent six months in Paris, most of her French had been learned when she was in French-speaking countries in Africa. She said she was never sure if she was speaking French with an African accent or not. Like a white person speaking English with a Nigerian accent, she would get a funny reaction from European French people. 'Or,' she said, 'maybe my French is just completely crap.'

I never got over thinking time with her was special and a treat. I can't imagine how much worse this grief would be if we hadn't become close again.

The release of the Greta Gerwig film of *Little Women* made me think about Annie. I much preferred the earlier versions from 1933 and 1949. Just thinking about them makes me want to stop writing and watch them right now. When I saw them as a child Annie was so clearly Jo — I was never sure who I was. I wasn't graceful or beautiful enough to be Meg or spoilt enough to be Amy, and I certainly wasn't nice enough to die quietly like Beth. I secretly wanted to be a Jo, too, and hoped I was. Could we both be Jo?

27

Empathy Overload

It's like a wrecking ball is continuously swinging into my stomach. That's how I felt at the news of the Manchester bombing and the Borough Market terror attack which took place within weeks of each other. If you're already grieving, these tragedies hit you harder: you are just so raw and open to emotion. I turned into one of those weeping women who went to Kensington Palace and laid flowers for Princess Diana. My empathy levels were probably certifiably high.

I was working in central London on the night of the Borough Market attack. It's an odd world when the first thing out of my mouth as the news started coming through was 'Let's hope it's just a huge traffic accident.' Obviously, a huge traffic accident is also horrible, but it feels more 'normal', it's not deliberate, it's a thing that just happened – a normal tragedy.

News started coming in as I was waiting backstage at the South Bank, at about quarter past ten. I walked back over Waterloo Bridge to Piccadilly for the late show at the Comedy Store. Audience members were talking to the doormen, explaining that they were leaving early to get home. Comics were told to keep the show tight and not mention anything. We weren't quite sure what we weren't mentioning, but we knew something had happened. None of the comics looked at their phones – it was better to go onstage not knowing.

Leaving my hotel the next morning, I wanted to give everyone I saw a reassuring hug. I got into the lift and a young couple got in with me. 'What a terrible morning,' I said. They mumbled something and didn't look at me.

I wanted to shout, 'Come on, people! Acknowledge what's happened! Let's connect as human beings! Let's spread the love and comfort each other!' Instead, I just stood awkwardly thinking 'what a terrible morning' hadn't quite been the right thing to say. Perhaps 'terrible night' would have been better? Or maybe 'sad day' was more fitting? The lift doors opened. Oh, they've gone . . .

At King's Cross I passed a Spanish lady who was looking exasperated as she talked to her daughter and waved a Tube map around. Here was another opportunity to connect, to do something, anything, to perform an act of kindness, to be useful. Yes. Lost tourists were perfect. I turned round and went back and asked if she needed help. From the look on their faces I must've launched into some very confusing directions. But the Circle, City and District lines are confusing. You get on a Circle line train, but the map inside will say District line. But it's maybe best not to try and explain all that to distraught tourists and then go into the whole history and tell them how the pink City line used to be the maroon Metropolitan line. Less is definitely more when giving directions. I could see the woman regretting letting me help her as I dragged her to the big map and started explaining the anomaly that is Edgware Road station. Her last words to me were 'Thank you for the rather Chinese explanation'. Which I assume is a Spanish idiom meaning 'shit directions'.

I had been in Manchester the day after the bombing at the arena. I know, I'm clearly a jinx. I was to play Sale in Manchester on Rory Bremner's tour and then double up to do a gig for a children's charity at the Comedy Store in Manchester, but I got an email from the manager on the morning of the gig telling me he had (quite rightly) decided to cancel the show. He was emailing all the ticket holders to ask them to go to the Manchester vigil instead. The Comedy Store is three minutes' walk from the town hall where the vigil was to be held. Manchester felt different to London after the attack, more vulnerable. The manager had been thinking of all the young staff who work at the Comedy Store, how it wouldn't have felt right to make them come in to work. He knew they'd need that night to recover. To be honest I had no idea who Ariana Grande was; I thought the newsreaders were pronouncing 'Grand Arena' in a strange European way.

Rory's show was a couple of miles from the centre of town. Only half a dozen people cancelled, and those tickets were sold to people on a waiting list. At first I thought it felt inappropriate to go ahead, but it wasn't. People had made the decision to come out, so, in that Vera Lynn way, we put on a show. Rory made a little speech at the start of the show about how our being together and laughing was the best thing we could do and how we shouldn't let these things change our way of life. Something has to be said at these times to relieve the tension, but once the elephant in the room has been mentioned, it's just a normal gig. A normal gig, but where you love every single person in the audience and there's a real bond. The members of the audience aren't sitting next to a stranger, they're sitting next to someone who, like them, chose to come out.

We gave all the money from ticket sales to the *Manchester Evening News* fund; it would have felt wrong to do anything else. It was the first thing Rory said to the audience, which made me laugh because obviously I wasn't going to say no, but a part of me did think, err, right, so no wages for me then?

I ran through my material in my head, just in case – you don't want to be mid-routine when you realise, oh shit, that punchline will seem in very poor taste after recent events.

Children died at a pop concert and the very next night we're laughing. That's the truth of it, and it plays on your mind, but I'm not a nurse or an emergency worker, I'm a comedian. The tram driver still drove the tram to Sale. The receptionist still checked me in at the hotel. Society heals itself by carrying on.

I remember doing a show in Birmingham on the night of 9/11. I'd watched it unfolding on TV in my hotel room, my husband and I talking to each other on the phone in disbelief, and I was sure no one would do a show that night. I was the support act for *Puppetry of the Penis* (if you're unfamiliar with their work, lucky you, it's actually worse than it sounds – there are no puppets). Two Australian men contort their penises and scrotums into various different shapes, then these are projected (in unnerving detail) onto a film screen behind them. I seem to remember a watch, a windsurfer and a cape being part of the repertoire. Surely it's not appropriate to come and look at men pulling their bits about on the day that three thousand people were killed in New York?

How wrong I was: we had a packed house. Whatever tragedy may happen, Brummie women will still want to come out and look at cocks (I think that was my opening line).

After Annie died I found this piece she had written. She was having a similar reaction, but for a different reason; hers, I think, was because she knew she didn't have much time left. It was the same feeling, though: an empathy overload. It's about the Romanian man she talked about in the hospice.

Atonement

I want to apologise to all the people I have passed in the street, day after day, and never had a conversation with. Well, some of them anyway. Perhaps not the people with axes in nighttime alleys. I would also like to say sorry to myself because before this Christmas Eve my wariness of strangers may have caused me to miss out on some great moments.

I have lived in London all my adult life, so of course I'm wary. A stranger might be dangerous, rude or just horrifically boring. People in cities are busy; I'm often very busy and can't be just chatting for the sake of it. It's better not to make eye contact on the tube, or start a debate at the bus stop, and definitely best not to ask men you don't know in the street what they are doing for Christmas.

The thing is, something happened to me on this last cold and rainy Christmas Eve to make me rethink the rules. It was an incident with a touch of an O. Henry short story about it. An incident of fleeting connection between strangers, which at least one of them will remember forever.

At the top of King's Road a man in a wheelchair, probably in his mid-thirties, has been selling *The Big Issue* every day for months. Being a mean, cynical Londoner I have to confess that I even doubted the wheelchair. But still, hard enough to sit out there in all weathers, so over the months I had bought from him, offhandedly, without more connection than a 'hello' and a 'thank you'.

As I went out this Christmas Eve to do last minute shopping, I decided to be festive and give him ten pounds without asking for change. He wasn't in his usual place. I found him sheltering from the filthy weather in the entrance to an arcade of designer shops.

He said 'thank you' twice when I told him not to give me change, although I noticed he didn't make eye contact. He had a strong accent but he'd been in London long enough to know how we are. Then, and I promise there was no Yule breakfast of mulled wine involved, I felt concerned for him. I asked, 'Do you have somewhere to go tomorrow?'

Steady, I wasn't going to ask him to celebrate Christmas in a tiny flat with my partner and me. I knew of a place near World's End that made a great effort to feed and shelter people over the holidays. All I was planning to do was offer benevolence at the end of a bargepole.

The man did something I really didn't expect. He looked right at me with a big, warm smile. It was as if his whole being lit up. He was surprised, pleased ... He said, 'This time tomorrow I will be on a flight home to Romania. By tomorrow night I will be with my children.'

He told me more about the children, his wife, how it had been eight months since he'd seen them. He was planning to get the last tube to the airport that night and wait for his plane. I gave him another ten pounds for coffee and snacks through the wait. If I'd been richer, maybe I'd have given him the money to get a taxi in the morning. And if you'd seen his face as he talked about going home, you'd have reached in your pockets too.

I wished him luck and walked away feeling so Christmassy and connected to the world. And very sorry that I'd never had the good grace to start a conversation with him before.

Since then I've been talking to strangers with fairly interesting results. My *don't look them in the eye, don't get involved* philosophy was a shrewd enough city survival strategy, but it made me miss out on a lot of people and I'm sorry about that. Of course, the next person I decide to talk to properly will be nasty, crazy or as cynical and suspicious as the old me. But I won't be sorry I tried.

Annie had had a few brain surgeries – and a lot of drugs – by the time she wrote that, so it's a little crazy, and some things don't make sense. The whole thing about him having a flight home seems very odd to me, which makes me sound like a *Daily Mail* reader: 'They're selling *The Big Issue* but they're all millionaires you know!' But I understand the sentiment behind it.

The whole encounter may have been dreamed up, but it's no less affecting for that. We all have notions about being better people or changing our ways; at least it means we are attempting self-improvement, no matter how temporary. Annie often had ideas about who she would be or what life she would lead, and then she would steer herself in that direction until she went off course, distracted by something else that interested her, or she was disabused of the notion – like when she wanted to take up horse riding in Spain. She saw herself in a crisp white shirt and riding boots, people in her Spanish village remarking admiringly, 'There's the interesting British lady riding again.' But then she got on a horse. Her verdict: 'Horses are completely uncontrollable and surprisingly small and spiteful.'

28

The Arseholes and the
People Like Us

Martin, me, Sarah and Molly on
Annie's bench in Battersea Park.

Five years after her death Annie still influences me. Is it strange to say I have gained things through her death? Maybe it's more accurate to say she left me gifts; she left me new people to help me. Her partner Martin and her friends Sarah and Molly. And, clichéd as it is, I do appreciate life more. I really savour a bright spring day or an autumn walk because I know how much she would have enjoyed them. I've just planted my daffodil bulbs and thought of her. The first daffodils have a special poignancy and joy – Annie always had fresh flowers in her flat and would rush out to get the first daffodils from the flower stall (although I think she fell out with the flower stall for being a rip-off and started going to the supermarket instead – that sounds like Annie).

I started running. I hadn't been running since I was at school, but I had to do something in the first year to help my mood. People said exercise releases endorphins and I needed a shitload of endorphins. Becoming someone who runs has helped me enormously. Just start doing it and in a year's time you will be someone who runs. Build up gradually. Don't be put off if you're slow or out of breath; it gets easier as you start to get fitter. At first I ran for a bit and then walked. Eventually I went from doing about 3k to doing 7k or 8k three or four times a week. A Nike running app is useful. It means that I know my distance and pace, but I'm only in competition with myself. It's the simplicity and the fact that I can do it anywhere I like – that and being outside. Gym running doesn't work for me. I get bored after 2k on a treadmill and want to stop. Where I live I can run down an old railway path and in five minutes I'm on Portobello beach, looking out to sea with music blasting in my ears. Do some sort of exercise and get outside; it really will help lift your mood. When I see other people around my age running, I think, 'I wonder *why* you're running? What happened to make you start running?'

Mindfulness, some people call it. I wouldn't. I'd have to punch myself in the face if I ever used the word 'mindful' . . . but I suppose it is really. It's appreciating the moment. My senses are somehow heightened; I get to have this day that Annie doesn't have. Rather than always being dragged down by the sadness, I'm sometimes buoyed up and able to really enjoy things more intensely. I love who I love more and don't bother so much with those I don't. For a while I was genuinely a kinder person, but I think that may have passed now – I can't help it, I have my sister's same irritability.

Annie would've totally been on my side with the young man in a coffee shop in Clerkenwell. Watching him as I waited in the queue, he looked like he hadn't even made coffee successfully in his own house, never mind being paid to make it for other people. There was a huge queue building up because of his ineptitude, and then he tricked me with a milk question and I gave an old person's answer.

'What milk do you want?'

'Err, semi-skimmed, please.'

'NO! Do you want almond milk, soy milk, oat milk or cow's milk?'

'Oh, just normal cow's milk.'

He could not have looked at me with more disdain (I now know that is an old person's answer).

'You really think it's normal to drink cow's milk?'

I somehow managed not to go 'oh, fuck off' although I really wanted to. He then explained, at great length, what fair trade coffee is. 'It's a more ethical way of doing business that ensures the small coffee grower gets a fair price for their harvest. It cuts out the big coffee companies. Are you okay with fair trade coffee?'

What a ridiculous question. Who wouldn't be? What kind of person is going to say, 'Fair trade coffee? I don't like the sound of that!' Who on earth would say that? Do you know who? Me. Because he pissed me off, I said, 'Um, do you have any coffee that exploits the coffee worker? You know, something where you can taste that they can't quite make a sustainable living – do you have any coffee like that? And can I get it with a dusting of cinnamon, please?'

Honestly, who hasn't heard of fair trade coffee? We're the fair trade generation FFS. He has no idea that, in the eighties, I was fighting in Nicaragua alongside the Sandinistas for the coffee workers. Well, I wasn't, but I bought The Clash's album.

Do you remember when we saw Joe Strummer in the Galleon café in Notting Hill, Annie? You always liked a cause – the Sandinistas, CND, Rock Against Racism, the PLO, the Women of Greenham Common, the Black Panthers, Free Nelson Mandela, Repeal Section 28, Stop the War – you really enjoyed a march.

Every judgement we made about people boiled down to a sort of instinct about whether they were our sort of person or not. It was also about fairness; a lot of Annie's judgements were about people who seem right but are actually very wrong, people who have something mean and unfair in them, people who are masquerading as nice people but who we know are really arseholes. Like when you meet someone who works for Amnesty International and you think, 'But you're a really horrible person, a narcissist and bully.' (True story.)

As always, Annie summed it all up in this piece.

Sports and Games – Just for Fun?

'Don't worry, you'll pick it up quickly, it's just a bit of fun,' my friends said, inviting me to go sailing with them.

The sun was glinting on the sea; there was a brisk snap in the breeze ... But I have learnt that there are several things nobody on earth does just for fun: assemble flat pack furniture, chiropody, or any kind of sport or games.

People you've known to be light-hearted, devil-may-care types for years will lure you into their shiny boat on the sparkling sea.

They'll promise you laughs, exhilaration and rum at sunset. What will happen instead is you'll get drenched and everyone will start barking orders at you as you find yourself strangled with ropes and impaled on a hook. Finally you'll be screamed at for not concentrating and spoiling it for everyone else.

Never mind an activity with potential for death by drowning like sailing; I've been screamed at for failure to concentrate in Buckaroo. Not a sport? Try telling that to the people who roared at me for putting Blu-Tack on the prospector's bucket. I thought such blatant attempts to cheat would amuse adults playing a game for five-year-olds. But no, there were people at the table who really cared if they won or lost.

I'm making these points as if someone out there might agree with me. This is silly of me, because experience is teaching me that my limited competitive spirit is just not normal. People start in with sports or games and become transported back through the evolutionary cycle to a time when we were all clawing and scratching in the primordial swamp to be the first one to grow legs.

I'd probably have been left behind then, too. I'd have been that lump of cells, lolling about in the ooze saying, 'Why's everyone shouting? I thought you said the evolving was just for fun.'

Time and again I've been at a summer picnic and somebody wrecks it by suggesting a game of rounders. We're in an idyllic setting, bellies swollen with many tiny snacks, people are chatting and laughing – but they're all getting uneasy, feeling they're frittering their lives away in non-competitive activity.

I say, 'No, I'm happier just sitting here.'

In fact I'd be happier just sitting there giving myself a bamboo manicure than playing rounders but no one ever believes me.

I say, 'But I can't hit the ball and I run like a hobbled camel.'

'It doesn't matter about that,' they cry. 'It's just for fun!'

They go on and on.

'If you really promise me it's just for a laugh,' I say.

'Yes, yes, we promise,' they lie.

And there I am: tricked, miserable on the outer field, getting screamed at for missing the ball as it flies past me.

Then everyone starts to turn on each other, arguing about who's out and who moved the cardigan marking second base. Soon followed by someone throwing the bat down, swearing, flinging themselves on the picnic rug and refusing to play any more. Or they stand at the sidelines shrieking that they've never liked any of us and they've slept with everyone's partners, twice. Then they stomp all over the profiteroles, take away the picnic rug, which is theirs anyway, and they are going home now, so there.

Not only do they provoke violence at the time, but sports and games also ruin friendships permanently. How can the profiterole stomper ever be welcomed back into the circle of friends? She may say, 'I didn't mean it and I was making it up about the partners.' But there will always be that shadow of doubt, caused by her, the rounders-cheating slut.

Similarly, when I pass my sailing friends heading off towards the marina in their bright coloured outfits, they pretend they haven't seen me. They're terrified I'll ask to come out with them again and I'll start hurling hysterical, tearful abuse because they've yelled at me for not reacting fast enough to some near-capsize incident.

They feel my behaviour in the boat revealed something about my character that's feckless, uncooperative, cowardly and irrational.

They don't want to be my friends any more.

There's the thing, the real purpose of sports and games isn't to bond people; it's to reveal their true characters. Where's the fun in that? Think about the times you've been shocked to find an apparently trustworthy friend hiding title deeds in Monopoly. Caught in their ruthless cheating, they'll kick over the board, weeping, telling you how much they've always despised you ...

So this is my advice: I am the only person to involve in sports and games if you really just want to have fun. And I'm not playing.

We shared a similar confusion about small talk. It makes me laugh to think about it. I could tell what she was thinking, the puzzled look on her face, the slight feeling of panic spreading through her body. Her eyes would dart about. *What are these people talking about and why? Are they seriously still talking about snorkelling?*

How to explain this? It's not subject matter – Annie and I have listened to our late auntie Mary discuss the church hall crockery for an hour and been riveted, but Auntie Mary could spin a tale. You have to earn your right to hold the floor.

It's also because we both have a type of shyness where we can't immediately just be ourselves. Our real personality retreats when we're unsure, hides away if we think people won't 'get us'. Also neither of us are any good at hiding our boredom. You know that feeling when someone is talking to you and you think, 'If they don't stop, I may have to start hurting myself, or them, but something has to happen to make this stop.'

Small talk is designed to make me feel like a freak. People around my age generally ask if you have children. When I say no a huge chasm opens up; they want me to fill that chasm with a reason, a story, an explanation for my child-free state, and I don't think it's any of their goddamn business. Ironically, this line of questioning makes me behave rather childishly, and I just stand there refusing to make the situation less awkward, like a toddler stubbornly refusing to answer a grown-up's questions. It also annoys me when people overcompensate and babble on about how great it must be not having children. No, it's not great. It's not that simple, now fuck off back to the buffet.

I know I have a fabulous gang of child-free friends to discuss this with, but it's not the same as discussing it with you.

Then, apparently, even weirder than not breeding is the fact that I have never skied.

'What do you mean you don't ski?! What never, ever?'

And then comes a whole list of things that mean I'm not a proper member of society.

'How come you haven't seen *The Lion King*?! What do you mean you don't like modern musicals?!'

'But everyone likes Queen!'

'Why aren't you interested in going to Australia?'

'You don't like barbecues? But they're great fun!'

'Oh, you like football – what team do you support? You can't just support "football", that doesn't make sense!'

'What do you do for a living? Really? My favourite show's

The Last Leg. You don't watch *The Last Leg*? How can you not watch *The Last Leg*?'

I remember foolishly trying to blend in by going to a drinks 'thing' near where we used to live in Morningside.

'So, have you read much Alan Titchmarsh?'

'The gardening man? Err, no.'

'Oh, you should. Can't believe you haven't read his stuff – you should give him a go.'

'Right. Yes. I will . . . when I've read all the books that have ever been written.'

The man then proceeded to lean in and tell me the plot of an Alan Titchmarsh novel; it apparently has some 'racy scenes'. He thought they were hilarious.

Aaargh, Annie! Why do people do that? We're not French; we can't do casual sexy talk. A completely humourless man who thought I was a completely humourless woman – which at that moment I was. Where was the joke?

'Sex! Ha, ha, ha!'

I don't get it.

He had a Range Rover. He liked his Range Rover very much, and he talked about it for some time before asking me what kind of car I had.

'A blue one.'

He and his silent wife stared at me. Yes, his wife was there when he did the sexy stuff. I know!

I tried to be more informative about my car. 'It's blue with a big dent in the front and scratches down the side because I just smashed into a Range Rover on the street outside.'

Nothing. Not a titter. They just edged away.

Oh, Annie, I so want to tell you these things.

Another thing Annie gave me after her death was discovering how much I enjoy being in my own head. I had always recognised it in her but not in myself. The piece she gave me to read at the funeral was the key. The description of how Norman Lewis reacted in social situations exactly sums up Annie in certain settings and what she thought.

'The reasons for his unsociability went beyond his reflex antipathy to the propertied English middle class (of which he was by now one). He had no small talk and he was temperamentally incapable of functioning at the casual sociable level of consciousness required for mixing with his neighbours. He felt the permanent diluted happiness of the middle classes to be the mortal enemy of his "intensely pursued private marvels". When the carceral boredom of a Finchingfield dinner party struck, his reaction was extreme. He described finding himself "with somebody like the local land agent on one side and the bank manager's wife on the other, and after half an hour I would physically feel all the power draining out of my body".' This is from *Semi Invisible Man: A Life of Norman Lewis* by Julian Evans.

Intensely pursued private marvels. That phrase went round and round in my head. That's what Annie had, these marvels that were to be taken out and played with and worked on. It's sad that there are marvels left unfinished, all sorts of marvels in various stages of germination that will never now get to grow. Annie can no longer enjoy her own private marvels. But up until near the end she did; that's why I say she could have enjoyed any kind of life – her brain could take her anywhere. It sounds simple, almost trite and Pollyanna-ish, but as life chucks shit at you, you realise what a gift it is to be able to enjoy your own thoughts, your own company. Like having a cheerful disposition, it gives you a fighting chance in the bad times. It wasn't like I'd never thought about this stuff before, but this was different somehow; it opened up to me the pleasure of spending time in your own head, the healing that can perhaps happen there. Writing has made me feel closer to her. I'm aware it's mumbo-jumbo nonsense, but it's comforting nonsense. To feel the drive and pleasure that I imagine she felt when she was writing and thinking up new ideas.

It's like a muscle memory, but it's not yours; it's theirs. I have it with my dad when I'm gardening, the feeling that I'm doing things the way he did them. Not even knowing how I know about gardening, I just seem to. That same love of tools and neat, weed-free grass as he had and calm, happy memories of my dad in the garden. Gardening is the one thing where I don't think when I'm doing it. I'm just totally in the moment. My friend Ben uses his dad's carpentry tools and feels the same, that it's him and his dad doing the job, a basic primal connection.

Catching Annie's face in the mirror, that's the weirdest feeling, looking at my face and seeing hers. It leaps out at me in a lift or when I walk past a mirror in a shop. At first it frightened me, although I don't know what I was scared of. You know in films when two people give each other a fright, then one screams and it makes the other person scream? I think it was just that, nothing very profound; I was scared that I would give myself a fright by seeing her face in mine. That I would always see it, so there was always a risk of getting a fright or of getting that pang at it not being her, it just being me. Lately, it's changed; sometimes now I see her face in mine and I think, 'There you are. Hello, Annie, nice to see you.'

At the hairdressers I told them about a bit of stand-up I

was doing on television presenter Holly Willoughby. Okay, it was less stand-up and more of a rant about how I don't get the point of her or that mindless enthusiasm that you see on *The One Show* and in light entertainment. There's something hard and flintlike behind that shininess, something conformist that makes me want to shout, 'Cock-sucking fascist!' Annie would have roared, but apparently the people in the hairdressers have never wanted to shout 'cock-sucking fascist' at a celebrity they didn't know, especially not Holly Willoughby. They said that Holly seemed like a lovely person.

'Of course she's a lovely person. I'd be a lovely person, too, if I had her life and lack of talent!' That's what I would've said to Annie, but I was at risk of getting a very bad blow dry so I shut up.

Annie, you would know that look that appears on the faces of 'normal' people when they don't get you and you've horrified them with your 'vileness'. And it's not actually that I have anything against Holly Willoughby; it's more that world. How hard and cold it seems when you are sad or low and someone on TV is smiling at you with their perfect glacial smile from their perfect happy life with their TV hair and make-up.

29

Annie Caulfield Tribute Fund

Backstage at our first Big Love, Big Laughs benefit at the
Comedy Store. John Bishop is taking the photo. Seann Walsh,
Ninia Benjamin, John Bishop, Al Murray, Dominic Holland,
Lenny Henry, Sebastian Ward, me, Stephen K. Amos,
Simon Mason and Steve Best with camera.

Everyone must think about their age when someone they love
dies before their time. Compare it. I am now older than Annie
was when she was diagnosed with lung cancer. I feel so young.

There's so much more work I want to do and places I want to go and fun times I want to have with fun people. Fifty-seven will be a big deal, and then fifty-eight will be a really big deal because that's an age she never was. Every year after fifty-eight is a bonus year. Recognising that is a positive thing, I suppose, another surprise that grief has left for me. Stop moping about and enjoy this year that the person you loved didn't get. Do something useful.

Collecting money for cancer charities (or whatever bastard disease is relevant to your loss) is an obvious and good place to start, and there is a great supportive community to be found there. It's full of people who, like you, have lost someone and is definitely something I would recommend getting involved in. Macmillan contacted me because I had done *Celebrity Mastermind* and nominated them as my chosen charity. I still can't believe I said to the lovely Macmillan women who rang me that I found the whole Macmillan coffee morning fundraisers nauseating and that the adverts made me scream at my TV, 'A fucking bit of cake doesn't make it better.' Then she told me how much money those coffee mornings raised and I said okay, but I still can't do that. Instead, I started doing a collection after my show every night at the Edinburgh Fringe. It was the Macmillan nurse who found the place in the hospice for Annie, advised her and Martin on so many things and helped stick Martin back together after each new and terrible phase.

For the first couple of years I mentioned at the end of the show that I'd lost my sister to cancer and I'd be collecting for Macmillan. What I didn't want was to do a funny show and then emotionally ambush the audience at the end. I am very conscious that mine is not the only grief, nor is it the worst grief. At the same time, I wanted it to be personal, so that people would maybe feel comforted by the fact that we're all in this shitty thing together. We're having a laugh, but who knows what sadness or worry people are coping with? And what if I burst into tears?

Luckily, I didn't cry – I said it as simply and as unemotionally as I could. Just the facts.

People have been very generous: there is now about £52,000 in the Annie Caulfield Tribute Fund. It was important to me to do it in her name; it meant she was still being useful. She'd like that.

A good friend of mine, the comedian Stephen K. Amos, lost his twin sister to cancer; see, mine is not the worst grief. By a strange coincidence – is there a word for the opposite of serendipity? – his sister had been in the Royal Trinity Hospice, the same one as Annie. Stephen and I shared a dressing room in Edinburgh, and when he saw me doing a collection he started doing one for St Columba's, the local hospice in Edinburgh. After the Fringe we got in touch with each other as we'd both been thinking of doing some sort of benefit gig for the Royal Trinity. It felt great to be in a position where we could do something to give back to them, a place I am so grateful to.

We hold an annual benefit gig at the Comedy Store in London and have now raised over £50,000. The night is called *Big Love. Big Laughs*, and we will do it for as long as we can get acts and an audience. It's usually on the first Monday in December – do look out for it.

The generosity of my fellow comics has been amazing. I couldn't sleep one night, so I got up early and thought, right, just ask every famous comic you have a contact number for.

I messaged Al Murray the Pub Landlord first. Ping. Two minutes later that was a yes. I couldn't believe it.

I kept texting.

Jimmy Carr – *yes of course, I'm doing another benefit that night so just work the times out with my agent.*

Graham Norton – *yes, but Christ knows what I'll do. I don't have an act.*

John Bishop – *yes.*

Katherine Ryan – *yes.*

Seann Walsh – *yes.*

Zoe Lyons – *yes.*

Ninia Benjamin – *yes.*

Omid Djalili – *yes.*

Jack Dee, Sean Lock, Joe Lycett, Tom Allen, all gave their time. And Lenny Henry, who I didn't know personally, said, 'Yes, I'll bring a band.' And he did.

The most precious thing to most famous people is their time; they are busy people. Lenny and his band rehearsed in the afternoon and then had to hang around until the end of the night to close the show. This may sound like some bollocks that Dolly Parton would say (I love Dolly Parton, by the way), but it really felt like there was a comedy family. The Comedy Store, a club that I have played for twenty years, bent over backwards to help us. If there had been some jobsworth making problems all the time, I think it would have been too hard on Stephen and me emotionally.

'Lenny wants to bring a five-piece band and backing singers – will that work on that four foot by four foot stage?' I asked Simon at the Comedy Store.

'No problem, Jo. We'll make it work.'

Al Murray did the raffle. I was honest and said to him that the raffle is the part of any charity night that really drags, so would he mind not doing his act and drawing the raffle instead? Some performers would have been miffed, their ego bruised – not Al. He went above and beyond and did the whole thing dressed in an inflatable Santa suit.

The charities do most of the work in terms of organisation; Stephen and I are just lucky that because of our job we have access to famous people. Why wouldn't we do it?

Stephen K. Amos and me onstage
before the benefit show.

Of course, only Martin and I were aware of the huge irony in people coming up and saying, 'Your sister would've loved it!' Well, actually, she would probably have hated it. She never went to comedy clubs. She didn't like stand-up.

But she would've loved giving back to the hospice where . . . I was about to say where she had been happy, and I know that sounds odd, but it's true . . . there were some bright moments of joy, and calm days and nights being cared for and soothed when so much was against her. Hospices, which rely mostly on private donations to function, are so important: what greater gift than to let someone die well? But fundraising is hard because they rely on legacies, and the downside of our living longer means people are now having to use that money to pay for care. One charity fundraiser said it was hard for the hospice movement because they didn't have happy stories. She then went on to say how the Cat Protection League were rolling in cash because they could show a picture of a cute kitten happy in its new home. I can totally see her point: what can hospices show? On their website I notice they're very careful not to talk about people dying. It's tricky when you can't actually promote what you do for your 'customers'. Annie wouldn't have wanted to see on their website that this was somewhere where she could 'die well'. Remember, it was 'a sort of spa'.

30

Déja Vu – Stripes

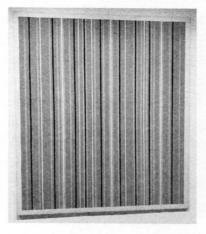

A Bridget Riley painting taken by me at
the Hayward Gallery, London.

Coincidence, fate, something 'meant to be' or random chance
. . . I don't know. I don't know why I suddenly wanted to go
and see some art at the Tate Modern. I rarely go to art galleries
(although the Tate Modern and the South Bank are two of my
favourite places in London). That brickwork is a work of art
in itself, and I love the bravery of its brutalism. It was made for
the people of Great Britain as part of the Festival of Britain and
it's stayed that way: it wasn't sold off to the highest bidder for
commercial development a few years later.

There was a Nam June Paik exhibition on. That sentence makes me sound terribly intellectual, but I'd actually never heard the name before in my life. For some reason I had a notion that when I was next down in London for gigs I would go and see some art during the day. His work looked right up my street. He made art using TV screens and homemade robots and tape recorders. He collaborated with musicians who played pianos that had dead keyboards. It was all utterly bonkers and very joyful. Paik actually coined the phrase 'information super-highway' before the invention of the internet; he saw the rise of TV and CCTV as a positive thing, a way of connecting people throughout the world and of mixing high and low culture. It's a bit like that Andy Warhol quote: 'In the future, everybody will be world-famous for fifteen minutes.' I always feel that a lot of people get the idea behind that wrong. I think Warhol thought that would be a good thing, an egalitarian world where everyone got to enjoy fame. (I'm very aware that there will be people reading this who know about art and are now rolling their eyes.)

Anyway, as I left the Tate and walked up towards the café at the Royal Festival Hall, there it was – *Bridget Riley*. The same retrospective that had been on in Edinburgh during the Fringe was on at the Hayward Gallery until the following Sunday. I was down again that weekend for work, so could go on the Saturday. I emailed Martin to see if he wanted to come with me. He said, 'Yes, let's do it.'

The exhibition was busy, and I was glad that we'd booked an early slot. The paintings make your eyes do weird things: you see prisms of colour in a black-and-white painting and curves and three dimensions on a flat canvas. I turned to look at one of her bigger works, and there she was. Sitting in a chair looking at one of her paintings was Bridget Riley herself. Some other people had also spotted her and gone up to talk to her. I whispered to Martin, 'That's Bridget!'

I circled around her. I didn't want to bother her, but I also kind of knew she wouldn't think it a bother; we were connected.

'Excuse me, Bridget. I don't know if you remember me, but you knew my sister Annie.'

I felt enveloped in her reply as she reached out for my hand and, holding it in both of hers, said, 'Of course I do, and I think about Annie so often. You do look like her. And she would have been here today; she always came to all my shows.'

I introduced Martin, and she told her friends that Annie was a writer who had been her assistant. She said so much in such a short time. It was exactly what you would want, for someone to remember vividly the person you loved.

'I used to put an advert in *Time Out* magazine for my assistants,' she told her friends, still holding my hand. 'I'll never forget when I opened the door and there was Annie with a silver suitcase and I thought, well, isn't she rather marvellous? I always wanted someone who actually needed the job, and Annie worked so hard cleaning and cooking. I was sorry to lose her. It's funny, I often quote Annie, but I've never credited her. In interviews I say, "You have to work hard to be an artist, harder than people think – it's work." I took that from Annie. She'd said that to me one time.'

I told her how I remembered the stripy paintings (the paintings from that period, 1980 to 1986, are called *The Egyptian Palette* – I think I even remembered to call them that).

She laughed as she told her friends how 'Annie had been

with me about six months, seeing these paintings every day, and one day she just said, "But, Bridget, they're all the same!" So funny, so refreshing.'

Martin and I went up to the next floor, and there they were, the huge stripy canvases that I had last seen being painted in the eighties. I looked at them for ages to see what the differences were (there are differences). When we went back down Bridget had gone.

Just seeing those paintings would have been wonderful — they were so familiar, so full of Annie to me — but for Bridget to have been there at the same time was too incredible. Martin and I kept saying, 'If that was in a film, you wouldn't believe it. You'd say, no, that's too corny. The artist wouldn't be there.' But she was.

I felt strangely happy and peaceful afterwards, like something had been completed. Thank you, Bridget. Thank you for being so gracious. And thank you for realising that Annie was special and 'rather marvellous'.

31

Queen of the Birds

Annie's writing had been changing in the last couple of years. Previously, she had travelled, so she'd written about the people she met and the places she went to; she wrote about people in history, told other people's stories – always a little outside herself.

But the play *Credit Card Baby* was the most personal work she'd written so far. As a comic I feel that it's only in my fifties that I have really found my voice. And my voice, it turns out, isn't that profound. My voice seems to joyfully enjoy telling the world to fuck off. I've waited a long time to find out, that's all I have to say.

You could always hear Annie's voice in her writing, but I think she was going to open up much more in her writing. We missed out on that, her future writing. I think one of the reasons her writing was changing was because she was happy, content. She would've been able to look at troubled Annie in the past and she would've used that, been able to go there.

And maybe, eventually, I would have stopped being the salt in her wound – or feeling I was the salt in her wound, as that view is totally from my perspective – or maybe that sibling stuff doesn't ever totally sort itself out, but you learn to muddle along. She was here first, and then my brother James and I muscled in. We get a very brief mention in Annie's book about Northern Ireland, *Irish Blood, English Heart, Ulster Fry*, and this is what she had to say about the arrival of her siblings: 'It worried me that they didn't have much to say other than "mine!". Usually about something that was mine. But siblings were small and could always be ignored.'

We'll all die; this is an everyday story, nothing unusual, really. Someone you love dies and then you feel bad. But whoever it is you miss, *is* important. If they're not, if we don't grieve, then what's the point? It's the Ferris wheel scene in *The Third Man* – all those little dots are important.

Having said that, there are also a lot of people wandering around alive and well who make me think, *really*? This woman talking absolute shite at the top of her voice on the train, she gets to live? And the man next to her, showing me his breakfast as he swills it round in his open mouth, he gets to live? Over Annie? If there is a God, then they're an idiot.

Recently, I saw an old friend, my boyfriend from my rockabilly days, Rocky, *The Lighthouse Keeper*, my first love (well, after Adam, so my first love who wasn't gay). Annie had been the only person left in my life who really knew him. Rocky used to look like Montgomery Clift, but now, although he still has the same handsome face, he also looks like I might be going to his funeral in a couple of years. It hurt to see him so changed – a beautiful and original soul who hadn't taken care of himself. Talking to Annie would've helped. I talked to her in my head. That Bukowski lifestyle takes its toll as you age. All that huge sad life stuff. Seeing him somehow concentrated that basic fact of life: there will be more sadness, and it will be sadder and harder to deal with without Annie. The ordinary, mundane heartbreak that getting older and losing people will bring, we won't go through that together.

And what a great old lady she would have been. What fun it would have been to have had 'tea and nonsense' together in our eighties. I don't know if I will live to be an old lady, but if I do, I will have to learn how to be one without her. There will be no footsteps to follow.

She would be mad as hell that she was dead; I think about that often. The Annie before she got cancer, she would be fucking raging to learn that she died at fifty-seven. But the Annie that had cancer, did she come to think differently? I still feel that awfulness in my stomach when I imagine what she felt, how terrible it must have been to face that, to face knowing you were dying.

I realise I'm lucky to have had comedy; it helped, because when I'm doing comedy I'm in a magical busy place, protected from grief. My comedy felt different – the worst thing possible was happening in real life, so I became fearless onstage. An audience can sense that, they like it; the comic should be 'the fool' who doesn't give a shit, saying what society is too polite to say.

And I'm still angry. Those adverts – we're walking over cancer. Fuck off, we're not. That's what I think every time I see them. They make me irrationally angry. Obviously, I want people to raise money for cancer charities, it's wonderful that people do, blah, blah, blah, but I hate those ads. They feel like a criticism of people who don't survive cancer, like a judgement. The dirty little secret that they don't want you to mention . . . people are still dying from cancer, every single day. The fact that cancer is a horrible, grotesque, merciless disease.

I know cancer is random and doesn't give a shit who it destroys, but sometimes I do get comfort from knowing that Annie lived long enough to be really happy; she had played the difficult hand well and was content and knew that she was loved. Had she filled the space she wrote about in *The Winners' Enclosure*? Maybe.

I think she had learned to look at 'the space' from a great distance, to see it as something far away, but it was something that could still harm her if she wasn't vigilant.

This is the piece of her writing we chose to have in the booklet that Woodrow put together for her funeral.

When I Grow Up

Oh no. Another week's gone by and I haven't changed the world. I hate it when that happens, don't you?

When I was a kid, I imagined my grown-up weeks would be filled with world-changing antics. I'd have foiled some major robberies and caught assassins. I wouldn't fly in through windows wearing a cape, nothing silly like that. These were realistic ambitions. I'd just have a way of looking at people to make them think: 'Oh, crime and evil just don't pay, she's right.'

I would stroll into laboratories and say to scientists, 'That cure for all diseases should have a bit more of the purple stuff in it.'

And I'd be right.

I would arrive at the ballet and hear the lead ballerina had broken her ankle. I'd say, 'I had a few classes, maybe I could try . . .'

Then I'd leap on stage, barefoot, and be astounding.

I would turn out to have a natural genius for most things.

And I would of course be displaying this genius while wearing diamond shoes and swishing my beautiful long blonde hair.

These imaginings filled my head at around the age when I also suspected that I might be Queen of the Birds. I don't know why birds specifically, except that we had a home festooned with house martin nests the summer of my sixth birthday and a tree in the garden topped with some other kind of nests. Birds of all shapes and sizes hopped around our lawn in the mornings and dive-bombed the trees at night.

I remember my mother commenting on the rush of birds to our house that summer. 'I've never seen anything like it, next door has a bird table and they don't get this level of bird harassment.'

Little did she know. I thought about telling her, quietly, modestly, that the reason for the bird population was the presence in our house of the actual Queen of the Birds; but I felt she wouldn't understand.

Just recently she bought a stone birdbath for her garden and when she showed it to me she said, 'I thought you'd be pleased, what with you being Queen of the Birds.'

Then she told me how she used to find my regal notes to the birds scattered all around the garden. 'I'd collect them up and save them. I must still have them somewhere.'

As Queen, one of my duties had been to write to the birds every day. I'd fold the notes and push them into the cracked brick outside my bedroom window. I was sure the birds were taking them, thus confirming my queenly status. It didn't occur to the six year-old me that they'd fall out of the brick, be blown around the garden and subsequently be scavenged by a nosy mother.

I couldn't remember what I'd been telling the birds. But my mother did: 'Oh, you were only six so they were mostly along the lines of, "Dear birds, hope you are well. I had chocolate custard today, your Queen."'

I've no idea where the Queen of the Birds notion came from, or went to. I now have no interest in wildlife and as for being a diamond-shoed superhero?

I don't even have beautiful long blonde hair. It's short, per-oxide streaked and more like a bird's nest than something belonging to a bird queen.

I live a contented but fairly unspectacular life.

The childhood me would be disappointed. Childhood me would be tutting and writing to the birds, 'Dear birds, yet again she's had a boring week. No chocolate custard, hope you are well, your Queen.'

Part of grown-up me would like to be more spectacular, but then again, spectacular lives seem tiring, dangerous and involve missing a lot of good television programmes.

Am I a disappointment to myself? Not really. For one thing, I no longer have all that pressing responsibility to the birds. Who never, it has to be said, showed any gratitude by flying down and carrying me away from school as I'd ordered them to in many, many notes. In fact, all they ever did for me was let my notes fall into my mother's hands. The bird notes made her worry I was lonely and she forced me into the Brownies. Which I hated. So, thanks, birds, don't come tweeting to me when you need help, you're on your own: I have more import-ant things that I'm not doing to worry about.

The calmer, contented Annie in this piece would've gone on to write differently. She always wrote in longhand first, and there were pages and pages of illegible scribbles in notebooks that will now forever be a mystery. Martin was able to edit and publish her last book, *My Cambodian Twin*, half of which had been written before she knew she had cancer. There is a subtle change in the focus of the book (she only fleetingly refers to 'going through cancer treatments'), but there is more of a searching for the moments of joy in life – not a Westerner looking for spiritual wisdom, not a huge life-changing moment, just an acknowledgement of small joys, small kindnesses. There are hilarious parts where she does do the usual Westerner-looking-for-enlightenment stuff and is quite underwhelmed, especially as her wise monk is a dead ringer for Eric Morecambe. 'He told me to seize the day. I had really hoped for more – or at least for the monk not to say things that everyone wrote on Facebook.'

I wanted there to be clues in the book, I wanted her to have written how she felt about cancer, I hoped to feel closer to her through the book, but it's not about her, it's about Sophea. Which is actually really irritating. It's hard to read when the real story to me is Annie. Try as I might, I can't care about Sophea. I wanted more Annie.

32

You Wore It First

The handmade taffeta dress that
Annie and I both wore.

Dread. That is what grief often feels like five years on. A feeling
of dread presses into me; my stomach turns as I wait for the
sadness to descend. It does pass. We all learn to live with it. In
fact I think part of us wants it, wants to feel that throb, like a
scar that aches periodically, keeping us close to them.

And then something monumental happens like COVID-19.
How can something like that happen and Annie not be here

to talk to about it? So often I said to myself, she would've *loved* lockdown – she wouldn't have had to go to any wanky meetings, she could've just been at home writing and playing with Martin. Going for big walks in Battersea Park or Hyde Park and loving the emptiness of her London, all to herself.

Life moving on is hard sometimes. Martin is dating again, which he should, and I wish him nothing but happiness, but it's hard because it means Annie's death is further and further away. And I can't move on. I can't have another sister.

Last year I walked the West Highland Way for Macmillan Cancer. It makes there seem a point to everything, it's my 'stitch in the cloth' (note to self: check the actual distance of the route before agreeing to do any walks in the future). I did it with friends and I was so grateful to them for doing it with me. We all got blisters and lost toenails, and my friend James broke three bones in his foot on day one but still finished the ninety-six miles. And we all managed to stay friends as well as raising £18,000 for the Annie Caulfield Tribute Fund.

Looking happier than our feet felt at the end of Walking the West Highland Way with Team McKeown for Macmillan Cancer Support. James McLuckie, Gill Gledhill, me and Sally Anne Hayward.

Maybe there's even a grieving for grief as her death becomes more distant. I know, aren't I just the misery that keeps on giving? It's a feeling that I am past the statute of limitations on grieving for a sister, that my time is up and people will roll their eyes. *God, is she* still *grieving her sister?* I don't talk about it, because it's selfish and boring to go on about it, especially as you get older and everyone has their own grief. Also Annie would hate to be the cause of me boring people. But, yes, I am still grieving. I am still sad for her. Still angry she isn't here. Still expecting her to be here.

Do you remember the blue gingham dress with the ric rac embroidery, Annie? Mum still has it. I found it when I was looking for old photos. We both absolutely loved that dress, despite its being a weird scratchy nylon material made in the days when no one worried about children wearing flammable clothing. It was strange to hold it and think of both of us wearing that tiny dress: you first, and then me.

There was a whole new box of old photos that Annie hadn't seen. James had brought it from my grandmother's house in Clonmel, Tipperary. She and her sister had returned to Clonmel from Belfast in 1968, and took over running their parents' store. We used to love visiting and playing shops behind the old counter. I found a photo of the shop with my dad and Grandma standing outside, and remembered Dad telling me they had gone south in 1941 when Belfast was bombed by the Luftwaffe. Here was the photo of exactly that time, my grandma's hand dramatically held to her forehead as though about to swoon.

My great–grandfather, my dad, my great–grandmother,
my grandma and great-uncle Jack outside the
family shop in Suir Island, Clonmel.

There are several large photos: some in frames, some mounted on cards. A row of ladies in white blouses and neat long skirts holding various guns, and behind them some handsome men smiling; in neat cursive writing it says *Irish Republican Army Tipperary 1916*. Photos of the famous 'Tipperary Flying Column', Sean Hogan at Dan Breen's wedding to Bridget Malone, these are well known stock photos in Ireland but it was a surprise that my dad's family had them in pride of place. It stirred a vague memory of a story great-uncle Jack told about running ammunition and messages from the shop in the civil war. Annie would have devoured these images.

One of many such photos mounted on card in my
grandma's house in Clonmel. Paramilitary women of
the Cumann na mBan (the Irishwomen's Council) and
IRA men at Billiard Castle training camp,
County Tipperary.

Also, scores of those posed portrait photos that people sent
back from America in the 1900s to show they were doing well in
the New World. And to show you were doing well, the women
wore huge hats with a random bird attached and no one smiled.
Ryans and Popes on Grandma's side of the family, and names
we'd never heard before: were they relatives or just people in
Philadelphia showing off? So many unanswered questions. As
James and I went through them we could hear Annie inventing
wild stories about great-uncle Jack and scandals as to why Aunt
Josephine never married. She would have shrieked with glee at
the strip of our grandma and great-aunt Josie messing about in
a photo booth, just sisters being silly in their sixties.

My grandma, known as Nan, and my great-aunt Josephine, known as 'Josie Lady'. This could have been taken any time from the mid-1960s to the mid-1980s – they always dressed like that.

Recently I dreamed about Annie. I have never dreamed about her before. It was so vivid it startled me, so like her that it pushed the last few years away. The sort of dream that when you wake up you're not quite sure where you are, and you need to recalibrate.

'Oh, please don't start telling people your dreams, Joey,' I hear her saying.

I was laughing as I looked at her in my dream. 'I thought you were dead . . . You're not dead?'

'Oh, I'm dead, but I thought I'd come back and see people.'

'But why with that hair?'

In the dream she had long hennaed hair, a style she'd had briefly in the late eighties when we all wanted to be Molly Ringwald. She didn't like herself with long hair.

'Oh my God, why did I come back with this hair? Joey, I've come back with the wrong hair.'

And she cackled with laughter.

How could she not be here any more?

Some Things

Here is a list of things that I associate with Annie. There's some empty space afterwards. You might want to write a list for your person or persons. It helped me. We spent some time together again.

black coffee
blue and white stripes
African teams in the World Cup
Rocket Dog trainers
white plimsolls
the smell of foundation
Jo Malone Lime and Basil
F. Scott Fitzgerald
Philip K. Dick
Youssou N'Dour
Pigbag
David Bowie
From Here to Eternity
Frank Sinatra as an actor
A Matter of Life and Death
fresh flowers
her hands

Timberland boots

Derek Jarman

tailored women's suits

Walter Mosley

Jim Jarmusch

James Baldwin

The Borgias and other gruesome TV series

the time we spent getting ready in a hotel room to go to an
    RAF function with James

Albert Camus

the ferry to Ireland

Calamity Jane

film noir

white jugs and navy blue glass

pasta with pesto and tuna

Oscar Wilde

my cousins

Noël Coward

David Essex

La Haine

The Intouchables

Toni Morrison

John Le Mesurier

coffee pots

John Lewis café

John Lewis

Refugee Council

Jean Rhys

how furious she would be about Brexit and what it's done
    to Britain

London buses
walking through London
the deck chairs in St James's Park
Earth, Wind and Fire
Gertrude Bell
Marc Bolan
Sinéad O'Connor
Battersea Power Station

Annie Caulfield, Writer

Annie wrote for film, stage, animation and television. She was a regular on Radio 4, contributing to *From Our Correspondent* and *Crossing Continents*, and appearing on lighthearted panel shows such as *Quote . . . Unquote* and *Off the Page*.

TV

Grim Tales 1989–1991

Josie 1991

The Real McCoy 1991

Lenny Go Home 1991

This Life 1997

Bosom Pals 2004

Chuggington 2008

RADIO PLAYS

Almost Always African (28/11/91)

After You've Gone (11/11/93)

Member of the Wedding (11/11/96)

Poisoned by a Tree (11/11/99)

Devil Take the Hindmost (14/2/00)

My Career Goes Bung (18/9/00)

The Truck six-part comedy series (10/1/01)

Summer 76 (10/1/01)
For Richer For Poorer (24/3/01)
Stage Mother, Sequined Daughter (29/7/02)
Passing (12/6/06)
Dickens Confidential: Captain Swing (23/5/07)
On the Field (10/9/07)
A Coup (28/9/07)
O Margate (2/10/08)
Your Only Man (27/12/08)
On the Field – Endgame (1/5/09)
The Von Trapps and Me (3/10/09)
Fact to Fiction (14/11/09)
On the Field – On Leave (28/9/10)
I'm Still the Same Paul (21/2/10)

BOOKS

Kingdom of the Film Stars: Journey into Jordan (Lonely Planet, 1997)
The Winners' Enclosure (Simon & Schuster, 1999)
Show Me the Magic: Travels Round Benin by Taxi (Penguin, 2003)
Irish Blood, English Heart, Ulster Fry: Return Journeys to Ireland (Penguin, 2005)
Travel Writing: A Practical Guide (The Crowood Press, 2007)
Writing for Radio: A Practical Guide (The Crowood Press, 2009)
My Cambodian Twin (Martin McNamara, 2019)

BOOKS FOR CHILDREN

Katie Milk Solves Crimes and So On . . . (Random House, 2006)
Katie Milk Solves Reality-TV Crimes (Random House, 2011)

Acknowledgements

Thank you to Martin McNamara for giving me permission to use Annie's writing. It seemed the one thing I could do that she would really have appreciated, to get people to read her work. As well as hopefully getting a sense of what an interesting and funny person she was. I can hear her saying, 'So the book's mostly about me? Oh, good.' Her work was also a good guide; I didn't reveal anything about her that she had not already written about. I am also grateful to Martin for many of the photographs used in this book, and for generally being Martin. I am glad to have you in my life.

I owe a huge thank you to *Standard Issue* magazine and particularly to magazine editor Mickey Noonan who gave me confidence and encouraged me. It's where I first started writing about this. The online magazine (now a podcast) gave me somewhere to share all my jumbled thoughts after Annie died. All the people who responded to those articles and got in touch – you are to blame for me carrying on. Reading your stories helped my grieving process, as well as encouraging my belief that what I was writing resonated beyond my own head.

Without Kevin Pocklington at the North Literary Agency there wouldn't be a book. Kevin emailed me about ten years ago asking if I'd ever thought of writing a book. Six years later

I replied to that email saying, 'I think I might be writing a book.' I was certainly writing, but it was Kevin who guided me into turning that writing into a book, asked the questions that made me think, helped me examine what I wanted to say. He also told me that he thought I would really like my editor at Polygon, Alison Rae.

There couldn't be a better editor for me than Alison. From our first glass of wine in the Tourmalet in Leith when we bonded over John Waters I knew this was going to be a person I could work with. She has made me feel safe and protected, which is so important in a book as personal as this. I've never had an editor before, so I don't know if it's unprofessional to love your editor, but I do: a wise and funny woman who feels like a friend and confidante I have had all my life. Most importantly I know that she gets and appreciates Annie.

When I had what I thought was a first draft of the book I knew I needed more help. I had written stand-up, radio shows and sitcoms but not a book. Was it even a book? Was it something anyone would want to read? I turned to a woman I had only met once, Annie's agent Janet Fillingham. I am extremely grateful to all at Fillingham Weston Associates for taking the time to get my first draft in front of Janet. And how incredibly generous Janet was with her time, reading the sprawling mess and then talking me through it for over an hour. Her advice and guidance undoubtedly changed the book for the better.

Thank you to my agent Vivienne Clore, who is a constant rock in my life – a rock being a good thing. There has never been an occasion when Vivienne hasn't been there for me. Vivienne also read the sprawling first version (the one that makes me cringe now), but as always she helped and supported me, knowing better than I knew myself that it would end up as something worth doing.

Now, this may seem churlish, but I notice in acknowledgements that people thank their family and friends; they thank them for their support and encouragement. I would like to apologise to my family and friends if I've made you feel you need to support and encourage me. How tedious of me. It seems very demanding to expect your loved ones to encourage you to write a book. I suppose I should thank my husband for leaving me alone so I could get on with it, but he was happily watching *The Walking Dead* and dealing with the zombie apocalypse.

There are family and friends who supported me and propped me up through the whole process of losing Annie, but it is dangerous to write a list. What if I forget someone? Whose name do I put first? So, in no particular order, Margaret Caulfield, Gill Gledhill, Adam Warnes, Molly Warwick, Yuen Wei Chew, Frances McKeever, Sarah Daniels, Stephen K. Amos, Jo Jo Sutherland, Sheena Anderson, Bruce Devlin, Sally Anne Hayward, Susan Murray, James McLuckie, Pauline Macmillan and Elaine O'Halloran.

The friend who I have bothered and burdened with this book is Jane Walker. I owe a massive debt to Jane for being a sounding board, a proofreader and a good friend.

And, finally, to my brother James to whom this book is dedicated. He gave me his approval and trusted me to write my version of our family. I am hugely grateful to him for that and for so much more.

I will make a contribution of all profits I receive from the sale of this book to Macmillan Cancer Support.